Modern Fly Fishing

Modern Fly Fishing

Complete Angler's Library™
North American Fishing Club
Minneapolis, Minnesota

Modern Fly Fishing

Library of Congress Catalog Card Number 93-84838
ISBN - 0-914697-56-0

Printed in U.S.A.
1   2   3   4   5   6   7   8   9

The North American Fishing Club
offers a line of hats for fishermen.
For information, write:
    North American Fishing Club
    P.O. Box 3403
    Minnetonka, MN 55343

Contents

Acknowledgments

The North American Fishing Club would like to thank all those who helped create this book.

Wildlife artist Virgil Beck created the cover art. Artist David Rottinghaus provided all illustrations. Photos, in addition to the author's, were provided by Virgil Beck, Lou Bignami, Soc Clay, Paul DeMarchi, Lefty Kreh, Complete Angler's Library Managing Editor Ron Larsen, Scott Ripley and Dale Spartas. The Fly Angler, located in Fridley, Minnesota, supplied tackle and equipment for several photos; thanks to store manager Dan Larson.

A special thanks to the NAFC's publication staff for all their efforts: Publisher Mark LaBarbera, *North American Fisherman* Editor Steve Pennaz, Managing Editor of Books Ron Larsen, Associate Editor of Books Colleen Ferguson, Desktop Publishing Specialist Ken Kaiser and Editorial Assistant of Books Victoria Brouillette. Thanks also to Vice President of Product Marketing Mike Vail, Marketing Manager Cal Franklin and Project Coordinator Jay McNaughton.

About The Author

Jim Casada, a native of the Great Smoky Mountains, grew up in Bryson City, North Carolina. He was raised in an angling family and began his fly-fishing apprenticeship at the age of six under the watchful, patient eye of his father. Since then he has used fly-fishing techniques from Alaska to South Africa for both freshwater and saltwater species.

He teaches fly fishing during the summer in both the Smokies and the Teton Wilderness Area in Wyoming. Jim has written about several fly-fishing-related subjects in many regional and national magazines. He writes the "Trout & Salmon" column for *North American Fisherman* and is the Profiles editor for *The Flyfisher*. In 1988, the Federation of Fly Fishers recognized Jim with its Arnold Gingrich Memorial Award and an honorary lifetime membership for his contributions to the literature of fly fishing. He has also won nearly 20 awards for writing and photography on state, regional and national levels. Jim is a member of the Outdoor Writers Association of America, and is an officer of the Southeastern Outdoor Press Association.

In addition to his interest in fly fishing, he writes about several other outdoor subjects. He is editor of *Turkey & Turkey Hunting* magazine and senior editor of *Sporting Classics*, and he holds masthead positions with six national publications. Jim also edits book manuscripts for several different outdoors series and topics.

Along with his varied outdoor interests, Jim is a professor of history at Winthrop University. He has authored several books on African exploration. Jim also was a founder and director of the university's soccer program. He has a bachelor's degree from King College; a master's degree from Virginia Polytechnic Institute and State University and a doctorate from Vanderbilt University.

"My true consuming passions," he says, "are fly fishing and turkey hunting. Both seem to have established firm holds on the corners of my soul."

Dedication

This book is dedicated to those understanding family members who know so well that fly fishing has been a bright thread running through the fabric of my entire life: for Dad, my mentor, who introduced me to the sport's wonders and guided me through my apprenticeship with the perfect blend of patience and persistence; for Mom, who served as a streamside pick-up and delivery service throughout my adolescent years and has always enjoyed the culinary pleasures afforded by my angling; and for Ann and Natasha, who have tolerated long trips and longer tales with good cheer. You have all brought joy to my angling days and meaning to life's ways.

Foreword

Challenge. If there is one word that describes the appeal of fishing to NAFC Members and other top anglers, *challenge* would be it. *Fun* is another great word that describes the sport of fishing. What could be more challenging and fun than taking a lunker on a bending rod and a tippet with a diameter that is as thin as the horsehair from which it once was made? Fly fishing has an active and growing following; its attraction is based on a number of different factors.

Fly fishing is by no means a new sport; in fact, it is quite old. Over the centuries, it has been identified with the elite—a "gentleman's" pursuit. Fortunately, as author Jim Casada points out, fly fishing is now shedding its elitist label much like a caddis fly sheds its case.

Many of you may have tried fly fishing. Perhaps you didn't continue practicing the sport because you didn't feel comfortable using a fly rod and reel. Perhaps you were discouraged in learning basic fly-fishing skills because the books and magazines devoted to the topic made it sound too complex. That's why we asked Jim to clear away the smoke and show NAFC Members that fly fishing can be easy to grasp and a lot of fun!

Obviously, no one buys a fly-rod outfit, some line and a few flies and becomes an expert fly fisherman on the first cast. It's a little more complex than that; however, it is not as difficult as its reputation implies. This book will help get you started on the right track to becoming a proficient fly fisherman.

You'll find that reading *Modern Fly Fishing* thoroughly is well worth the effort. For example, you may be surprised to learn how many different species of fish can be caught on a fly rod. Trout and salmon have long been the targeted fly-fishing species, but they are by no means the only species susceptible to flies. Imagine the fun and excitement of taking a large northern pike or muskie on a fly rod. That's a challenge that will keep you reliving the event for years to come. If you're looking for a peaceful evening with lots of action, try wade-fishing a farm pond loaded with bluegills. You will have a ball working a small popper on the surface!

Whether you want to become an expert fly fisherman or merely proficient enough to enjoy another way of taking fish, this book will help you do it. Jim has fished with a fly rod for years and understands that many NAFC Members want to add new approaches to their growing arsenals of fishing weapons. He recognizes that many NAFC'ers may not consider fly fishing to be an all-consuming passion. Instead, it may be just another way to enjoy their favorite sport—fishing.

Jim starts by detailing some of the sport's rich and colorful history, then describes in detail the necessary tools for enjoying fly fishing to the fullest. From experience, he knows what equipment you'll need, what lines are best for certain situations and what problems you'll most likely encounter.

After leading you through the selection process, he directs your attention to the basic fly-fishing cast you'll need to master. Then he'll teach you other challenging casts used in certain situations on the water.

Most anglers probably use just two or three basic knots in fishing; however, fly fishermen will need to master more. Jim has chosen proven performers and explains how to tie them.

There are many fish species you will want to tackle when you've mastered fly fishing's basic skills; however, Jim recommends starting with panfish because they're "exceptionally cooperative." Panfishing allows you to practice and fine-tune your skills before attempting to take more challenging species, which require stealth and spotting abilities.

This book also recognizes the increased use of fly rods for various saltwater species. Fishing tidal basins and flats for tarpon, permit and other species that invade these areas to feed are popular strategies. Jim also talks about taking billfish on fly rods, a feat that does not come easily.

As you can see, *Modern Fly Fishing* is packed full of tips and information that will make fly fishing an exciting addition to your fishing skills. I'm excited about this book and certain that you will be, too.

Good fishing!

Steve Pennaz
Executive Director
North American Fishing Club

Getting Started
In Fly Fishing

1

Fly Fishing:
Every Person's Angling

aving an incredibly rich and varied past, fly fishing dates back as early as classical Rome where various commentators mentioned catching fish on hooks decorated with feathers. Even literature devoted specifically to the recreational pursuit of fly fishing can be traced to the late Middle Ages when Dame Juliana Berners' book, *The Treatise of Fishing with an Angle*, appeared in the 14th century.

If Dame Juliana is fly fishing's godmother, Izaak Walton is its patron saint. No name in the history of angling in general is more widely recognized than this venerable 17th century Englishman's. His book, *The Compleat Angler*, has gone through approximately 500 editions. Walton, however, is not mentioned very often so only a few anglers know the man and his work. Therefore, it is worth sharing a few of Walton's words of wisdom. He reminds us that the true meaning and significance of fishing involves more than the act of catching. He also stresses that simplicity is the essence of fly fishing.

Walton's views of angling were straightforward and timeless. He stated that "angling may be said to be so like the mathematics that it can never be fully learnt." Yet who would want to spend free time in pursuit of a sport which promised complete mastery? Today's fly fisherman finds the recreation, as did Walton, "an employment for his idle time, a rest to his mind, a cheerer of his spirits, a diverter of sadness, a calmer of unquiet thoughts, a moderator of passions, a procurer of contentedness."

Fly fishing can be relaxing and simple for the beginner yet challenging for the advanced fisherman. The pristine water and beautiful scenery are just some of the sport's advantages.

Fly Fishing: Every Person's Angling

For those who seek contentment, traveling to the water for the day may be the answer. Walton says, "angling is so pleasant that it will prove to be, like virtue, a reward to itself."

One of the most interesting things about Walton was his unassuming nature. He was, for one thing, quite ready to use bait on occasions—a fact which purists sometimes conveniently overlook when evoking his name. Yet who can help but chuckle at his instructions on the best way to handle a frog being cast for pike: "Use him as though you loved him, that is, harm him as little as you may possibly, that he may live the longer."

The Pitfalls Of Elitism

Today's fly fishermen need to be reminded of Walton's down-to-earth nature and common sense, which characterized his outlook. He never fell prey to taking himself too seriously. Fly fishermen have been guilty of precisely this sin. (The sport's leading spokesmen have often been unabashed elitists.)

This high and mighty attitude began in 19th-century England when the sport was considered the exclusive preserve of wealthy gentlemen. Some thought the only proper way to fish was with the wet fly; others were equally vehement in proclaiming the exclusive virtues of the dry fly. There were endless arguments about the ethics of fishing upstream or downstream. These attitudes were arrogant, intolerant and generally unmindful of the fact that fly fishing should be, first and foremost, fun.

When fly fishing became popular in America, many of these attitudes prevailed. Arnold Gingrich, the author of *The Fishing in Print* and one of the finest writers on fly fishing, described these early American fly fishermen as "pompous, conceited, opinionated, and more than a little stuffy." Several other writers have said the same thing.

Today's fly-fishing student will encounter esoteric books and articles, full of Latin names for insects and hinting at tactics and techniques which are suitable for use only by the select few. When this happens, he is likely to throw up his hands in despair. Even his good friends will give him misleading information. Having already achieved some degree of familiarity with fly fishing, they toss about incomprehensible terms, repeatedly implying that the doors of fly fishing's portals do not open for ordinary mortals and generally going to inordinate lengths to say how incredibly diffi-

Fly fishing's history is full of myths about the sport's complexity and requirements for participating. In reality, fly fishing is a sport for all skills and all ages.

cult the sport is. Let's say right now, emphatically and without any equivocation whatsoever, that such attitudes are hogwash!

Most modern fly fishermen know better, and those who don't are masters of self-delusion. Still, old attitudes of elitism and tendencies surround fly fishing with a near-impenetrable cloak of mystery die hard. The sport has somehow evolved as one surrounded by myths; however, in reality, it is no more intricate or complicated than any other type of fishing. When reduced to its essentials, fly fishing is comparatively simple—not highly complicated.

It's All Really Simple

It does not take a world-class athlete to learn to cast satisfactorily, nor does it require a towering intellect to acquire the basic knowledge of equipment and one's quarry to catch fish. With those considerations in mind, one of the most important things you can do as you move into the meat of this book is approach fly fishing with an open mind. Forget all the things you have heard about it, including the incredible difficulty or the outrageous expense in getting started. Instead, look upon fly fishing in a relaxed, easy going, "I can do it" manner. That outlook is fully justified because you can do it.

Fly fishing is a sport for all people and all seasons—one which will repay those willing to take the relatively easy steps required to learn its rich, lasting rewards. The approach adopted here emphasizes simplicity and practicality. It is possible to be casting well enough to catch fish with only a few hours of work. You should also know that a person just getting started in fly fishing can acquire a basic but serviceable fly-fishing outfit for only $200. Better still, no matter where you live in the United States, you will most likely be within an hour's drive of water suitable for putting that newly purchased outfit into action.

Fly fishing, though relatively uncomplicated in its essential elements, is distinctly different from spincasting or baitcasting. The equipment, approach and, yes, even the prevailing attitudes of fly fishermen are at variance with other common fishing techniques. For starters, competitiveness (except with the fish) should not be a factor in the sport. Nor should you approach fly fishing determined to measure your success solely in terms of numbers of fish caught. If you spend several hours on the water, catch a few fish and end the day both exhausted and exhilarated, you are well on your way to discovering fly fishing's deeper meanings.

Certainly fly fishing deserves its description of being the "contemplative man's recreation;" however, the contemplation it brings soothes the troubled soul and pushes worldly cares into the background. That should be what you seek from fly fishing—inner peace and contentment. If you can adopt this sort of philosophical outlook, you already have taken a gigantic stride toward becoming a fly fisherman.

You can expand your fly-fishing knowledge and experience to a great degree because the sport does have a lot of complexity. However, that complexity comes after the fact, if at all. It comes after you have acquired the basics, after you have had a meaningful taste of fly fishing's joys and, most of all, after you have already caught fish.

Fly fishing is comprised of many layers of achievement. As you acquire the skills necessary to peel off each layer, new challenges await you. Far from being intimidating, each fresh challenge is welcome because it can be met at your own pace and in your own way. This book is intended to guide you as you move into fly fishing. For those with no previous familiarity with the sport, it will serve as a primer, a step-by-step guide to all aspects of fly fishing. It should be equally useful as a reference source for those already reasonably accomplished in fly fishing.

Most of all, remember that fly fishing is meant to be enjoyed. If you keep the "I can do it" attitude in your mind at all times, fly fishing is a wonderful window of opportunity.

2

Rods And Reels

L ogically, the first place to start when it comes to fly-fishing equipment is the rod and reel. A good rod will make casting smoother and swifter. A suitable reel provides easier casting and finer fishing, too. The rod and reel are, along with line, leader and fly, the essential components involved in fly fishing.

The fly rod's function is to send the line and fly to their intended destination. It is an extension of the angler's arm. The longer the rod, the more leverage for casting; added length means a longer casting arc. The rod does more, however, than extend one's reach and reduce the effort needed in the casting stroke. Its bending capacity, or rod flex, acts as a spring. The line loads the rod, making it bend. (More details on this subject are in Chapter 7.) The rod then returns to an unbent position, helping catapult the line through the air during the cast.

In short, the rod does three basic things: It extends the angler's reach and leverage, flexes with line weight and straightens itself out. These rod functions enable the angler to make a cast. The rod's performance in these functions determines the fisherman's casting performance.

Fly-Rod Materials

The backbone of any fly rod is the rod blank. The materials which make up the blank are critical in determining just how well a rod will perform. Virtually all fly rods—whether new, used or

The fly rod is basically an extension of the fisherman's arm which helps get the line and fly to their targeted destinations. Rods basically do three things: (1) extend the angler's reach, (2) flex with line weight and (3) straighten out.

Rods And Reels

true antiques—will feature blanks made of one of four materials: bamboo, fiberglass, boron or graphite.

Bamboo. Split-bamboo fly rods are richly steeped in tradition. They are made from cane or bamboo. (The best raw material is grown in Asia's Gulf of Tonkin region.) Slender, straight bamboo poles are cut, cured and milled into tapering strips on a machine. These form the basis for making the blanks for bamboo rods. Usually six strips are glued together to form a hexagonal rod blank; however, other configurations, such as the "quad rod" (four strips) or pentagon (five strips), are seen on occasion.

Making a bamboo rod involves several steps, including guides, grip and reel-seat installation, sanding and varnishing. Almost all of this work is done by hand; therefore, bamboo rods are expensive. This is especially true for a really well-made, high-performance bamboo rod. You can sometimes find older ones fairly inexpensive; however, they are likely to be either limber as a buggy whip or unresponsive as a hoe handle. In both cases, attempting to cast with them is an exercise in futility.

Still, many experienced fly fishermen insist on using bamboo, and their reasons go well beyond being confirmed traditionalists. No synthetic material can come close to the warmth and beauty of bamboo, and the action of bamboo gives exceptional "feel." Bamboo rods—whether custom-made, modern ones or well-preserved, functional ones from the golden age (the first 40 years of the 20th century)—are almost certain to increase in value in years to come. A fly rod should not be viewed primarily in terms of investment value; however, it is comforting to know that a rod you cherish also has excellent growth potential.

There are some limitations, too. Bamboo rods are fragile. A heavy streamer banging against varnish can do some real damage—bamboo doesn't handle heavy flies well. Constant high stress from casting big streamers or even popping bugs can put a "set" or permanent bend in the rod. Tips of bamboo rods are easily broken, and they are much more difficult to replace than those made of other materials. That is why many older bamboo rods came from the maker with an extra tip. Obviously, bamboo is fragile and requires extreme care.

The "beginner" fly fisherman should not use bamboo unless he has a hand-me-down rod. Even then, however, the rod may provide inferior performance or be too valuable for a novice's rough

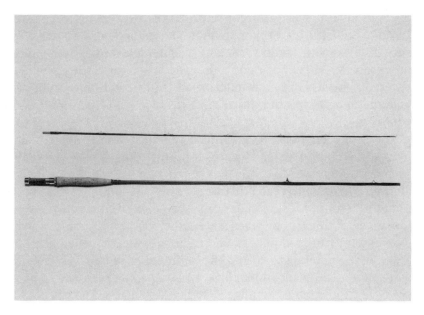

Bamboo rods are usually handmade and quite expensive. They offer beauty and tradition yet are extremely fragile. This custom-built bamboo rod is on display at a fly-fishing specialty store.

handling. As the angler's interest and ability develop, it is always possible to turn to bamboo.

Fiberglass. Fiberglass rods became quite popular in the early 1950s. Even though they lack the beauty of bamboo and the performance of graphite, there are some advantages to using fiberglass rods. Probably the most significant point is that they are inexpensive. The earlier models of fiberglass rods were far inferior to later ones; if you find one and purchase it at a flea-market price, it may actually be a piece of junk. Fiberglass has been largely replaced by space-age materials; however, rods made of this material still have the virtue of being readily mass-produced and thus cheaper. Fiberglass is also very sturdy. If you choose a fiberglass rod, make sure it comes from a reputable fly shop, not a general sporting goods dealer. If acquiring a used fiberglass rod, check its flexibility and recovery time (how quickly the rod returns to normal after being whipped) and do some casting with it. Glass rods have notoriously slow actions, which makes mastering the casting process more difficult.

Boron. To a considerable degree, boron's popularity has decreased like fiberglass's. Today, most quality rods feature well over 90 percent graphite content. Boron is even lighter than graphite, which is exceptionally light. That allows one to make a very thin rod with boron yet retain the strength needed to handle line properly. Many boron rods proved capable of casting several different line weights reasonably well. Still, graphite is the rod material of today, possibly with small percentages of boron blended in.

Graphite. The keys to graphite's popularity are strength and lightness. Graphite also features a high degree of elasticity; it "dampens" (returns to straightness) rapidly after being flexed. This characteristic is a great advantage when it comes to casting. Graphite technology has changed dramatically since rods were first made of this carbon fiber material in the 1970s. This has led to ever-improving rod quality, and it has also meant availability of a welcome price range. Although the finest graphite rods remain quite expensive, you can purchase an acceptable rod made of 95- or 96-percent graphite for under $100.

Graphite rods are undoubtedly the rods for fly-fishing newcomers. The price you pay and the rod you select will revolve around features other than the blank. Remember that many different rod manufacturers use precisely the same blanks, yet their rods vary widely in price. One reason for this is brand name; another is because different quality components were used to turn the graphite blank into a finished product.

Filling In The Blanks

Guides. Guides are used to direct the line from the lower or butt section of the rod to the tip. Snake guides, which have serpentine shapes, are normally used on fly rods. The exceptions to this are the first, last and keeper guides. These three are all special-purpose guides. The keeper guide, which is located just above the grip, is simply a place to hook the fly when the rod is mounted but not in use. The top guide fits over the rodtip. The bottom guide, sometimes called a stripping guide or butt guide, often has a ceramic interior and is of the ring type common on casting rods. All fly-rod guides should be of top-quality metal, and some are often chrome-plated. They should also be well-wrapped and spaced fairly close together.

Three dead giveaways to a rod of inferior quality are cheap guides, poorly spaced guides or guides with inferior wrapping.

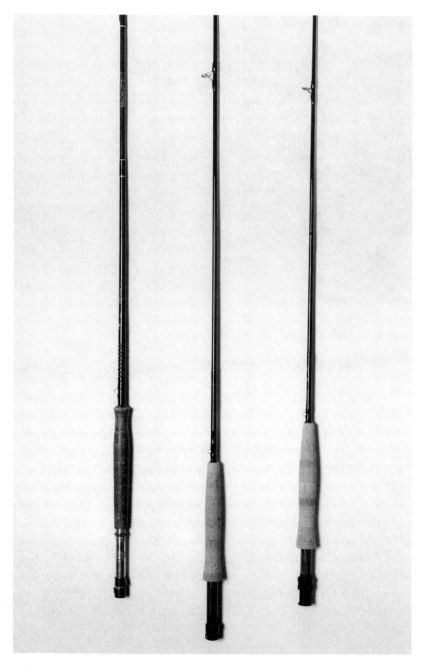

This trio represents different materials used in manufacturing rods. The rod on the left is made from fiberglass; the middle rod is made from boron; and the rod on the right is made from graphite, the most popular material in modern fly-fishing rods.

The keeper guide, also known as the hook holder, is located above the grip. It holds the hook in place when the rod is not in use.

Cheap guides will most likely be painted gold or silver or have a rough appearance. Make sure the guides are the proper size to allow line to flow through them easily and smoothly. You can normally discern a shoddy wrapping job when looking at it. The wraps should be well-covered with epoxy or a top-quality varnish, and the wrapping threads should not extend any great distance. If they do, they will detract from the rod's action. When it comes to the correct number of guides, a simple formula can be used to determine whether the right number is present. There should be a guide for every foot of rod length, plus one. Thus a 7-foot rod should have eight guides. If the number is less than this, the line will slap against the rod during the casting motion, reducing the rod's effectiveness.

Ferrules. The ferrule is the joint where two sections of a fly rod come together. Traditional, high-quality bamboo rods normally carry metal ferrules of a silver/nickel blend. For graphite rods, most of the blanks are formed so they marry at the ferrule without any extra material. This makes for smoother rod action; however, loose fits or a ferrule "blowing out" can be a problem.

The Grip. Virtually all grips (or handles) on fly rods are made of cork. Cork handles are formed from hollowed-out rings of cork which are simply slipped over the rod blank and glued together.

Fly-rod grips come in many different designs. These include the rounded, rather small grips (sometimes called "cigar grips"), the more dramatically tapered grips (called superfine grips), grips with flattened space at the top to accommodate the thumb, grips which bulge noticeably in the middle and many others. When you're selecting a grip, the most important thing is that it is comfortable in your hand.

Reel Seat. The reel seat is the device used to hold a reel at the rod's base. This is usually done with sleeves—one fixed and one movable—which slide over each end of the reel base. The movable slide is locked in place by rings which screw tightly. Depending upon the direction in which they lock down, reel seats are described as being up-locking (the ring turns toward the rodtip) or down-locking (the ring turns toward the rod butt).

This down-locking reel seat holds the reel at the rod's base. The rings used to lock the movable slide turn toward the rod butt.

Either way works fine, although letting your hand drift too far down on the grip can loosen down-locking seats or cause a blister to form on your palm. The hand belongs at the back of the grip when in proper casting position so this is an important consideration. However, double rings, which are found on many reel seats, will generally solve this problem on down-locking seats.

Occasionally, you will find a reel seat which has no true locking device at all—just two circular slides or rings to slip over the feet of the reel. These are most frequently encountered in tiny rods in the 1-, 2- or 3-weight class. They are not recommended because the rings never fit tightly; they constantly need to be slid back or they'll slip off the reel seat. Avoid them if possible.

Choosing A Rod

Rods come in a number of different weights, ranging from 1 to 15. A 1-weight is a diminutive fly rod used on small streams or in other situations where short casts are satisfactory; a 15-weight is the heaviest saltwater rod available. For those just starting out, a 6- or 7-weight rod will suffice; however, fish species and type of water will play major roles in the selection process.

One- through 4-weight rods are light and delicate. They are primarily used for panfishing, fishing for small trout and stream fishing. Rods in the 5- through 8-weight class are more versatile. They are used for most freshwater and smaller saltwater species in creeks, large rivers, lakes and the ocean. Nine-weight rods or higher are used primarily in saltwater; however, they are also used for powerful freshwater species, such as steelhead and salmon.

You will also need to decide on rod length. Standard rod lengths in the popular intermediate weight classes (5 through 8) are 7^1/$_2$ to 8^1/$_2$ feet. Most are two-piece rods; however, older three-piece bamboo ones exist, as well as four-piece pack rods. Modern pack rods perform just as well as two-piecers, and they are also quite convenient.

When selecting the appropriate rod length, you should keep several factors in mind. The shorter the rod, the greater the loss in casting efficiency. You lose some mechanical advantage as the reduced arc, through which the rodtip moves, decreases. On the other hand, long rods (about 9 feet or more in length) involve added weight and increased air-resistance. These can also cause a loss of efficiency.

The important thing is to be comfortable with the rod length you select. If you roll or distance cast a lot, a longer rod works best. For tight, overgrown streams or situations where delicate casts are important, a shorter rod will work better. For the average individual, an 8-foot rod is a good all-around selection.

Whatever your rod's weight and length, you must understand the rod's action. Pertaining to casting motion, there are three basic types of rods: tip-action, medium-action or full-action. You can determine the nature of a rod's action by holding the rod handle and whipping it vigorously through the air parallel to the floor or ground.

A rod with its flex toward the tip is a tip-action rod. Tip-action rods cast well in experienced hands, and they are often favored in saltwater because their stiff butt section allows anglers to put some real muscle into fighting powerful fish. On the other hand, that same "stiffness" in smaller weights decreases the enjoyment level for anglers fighting fish caught on lighter rods.

Medium-action rods will flex in the upper half of the rod. They cast beautifully and give the angler a real sense of "touch." Where delicate presentations and butt strength are important, medium-action rods are best. Most contemporary rods are medium-action because they offer optimum all-around performance; thus, most beginners should start with medium-action rods.

Full-action rods flex almost all the way down to the handle. Some bamboo rods, especially older ones, have this characteristic. Full-action rods are fine for delicate nymphing with a short line or handling flies size 16 or smaller; however, you cannot make long casts with them or fight large fish.

In selecting rods, stability is probably more important than action, especially since 80 or 90 percent of "off the rack" rods will be medium-action. A rod should dampen or stop vibrating quickly after being whipped firmly. While the rod is vibrating, it should move in the same plane. If there is variance in the plane of vibration or it "wobbles," the rod will not cast as well as you would like.

Finally, you should test-cast a rod if possible. Obviously, this cannot be done with mail-order or cheaper, prepackaged rods. If you are going to buy a more expensive rod, however, you should insist on some practice casting first. Most fine fly shops will allow this, and their sales staffs can give you some helpful tips on rod choice, too.

Rod Flexibility

Action, or flexibility, is an important element when selecting a rod. Rods that flex toward the tip are tip-action rods (top); medium-action rods flex in the upper half of the rod (middle); and full-action rods flex almost all the way down to the handle (bottom).

Fly Reels

A fly reel is simply a line-storage mechanism. For example, in freshwater fishing, the angler normally plays the fish with the off-hand (the one not used in casting) by stripping in line as the fish tires. This approach, however, does not work on big fish—even a 2- or 3-pounder on delicate leader material must be played on the reel. Otherwise, you will lose the fish. Drag becomes an important consideration in this situation. You can get a good, functional reel with an adjustable drag system for under $100; however, for big, high-performance saltwater reels, the cost will be much higher. As with rods, consider the type of fishing you will do most often.

The obvious first factor in selecting a reel is weight. It should balance with your rod. Thus a 4-weight rod should be accompanied by a 4-weight reel (and 4-weight line) and so on. Weight

A good reel with adjustable drag is important in fly fishing. This Browning 2078 is a popular model and sells for under $100. It is designed for 7- or 8-weight rods and lines.

information is normally provided on the reel. (Many times reels are denoted as being suitable for two rod weights, such as a ⁵/₆ or a ⁶/₇. If you do not know the reel's weight, set it on the rod and fill it with line. The balancing point for the entire outfit should be at (or extremely close to) the grip.

Reel Action

Most fly-fishing reels are single-action types: One revolution of the reel handle will turn the reel spool one time. Single-action is an established tradition in fly fishing. Even when whopping saltwater models are involved, it is the way most reels are designed. You can find multiplying reels, which are commonly used with bait- and spincasting rods, for fly fishing. These reels contain a gear mechanism giving the angler a mechanical advantage when the reel is cranked. A single full turn of the reel handle will produce more than one spool revolution. This can be helpful in areas where really long casts are involved or in situations where you need to strip off or recover a lot of line quickly.

Automatic reels, which retrieve line by a lever-activated spring rather than a turn of the reel handle, used to be popular; they made bringing the line back in simple. However, they have a number of disadvantages. They are heavy, causing the rod to be thrown out of balance; they do not have good drag systems; and they tear up easily.

Desirable Reel Features

Most quality reels have removable spools. When selecting a reel, make sure it has a removable spool and that extra spools are readily available. It is best to buy at least one or two extra spools when purchasing a reel. Extra spools carry extra line, preparing you for most situations. For example, one spool can hold a floating, double-tapered line; the second a sink-tip line; and the third a shooting head (covered in the next chapter).

Another useful feature is an exposed-rim spool. This adds extra drag with friction produced by placing the palm of your hand against the spool's rim as the fish takes out line. The technique is called "palming the reel"—it works great for fighting powerful fish.

When pursuing larger fish species, you'll discover the importance of the drag system. It should work smoothly under pressure,

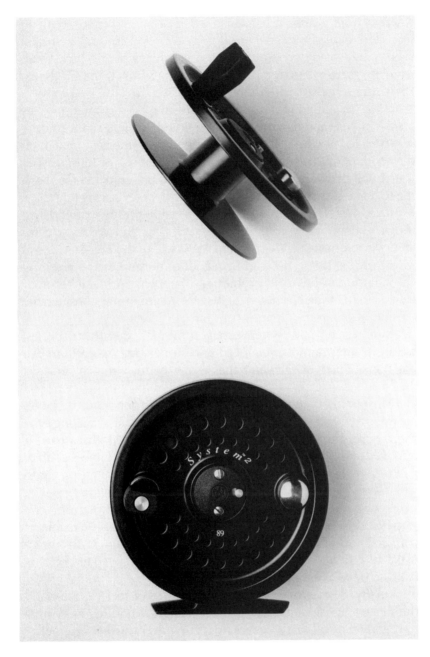

It is important to select a reel with desirable features. Some features include a removable spool, adjustable drag system, exposed rim spool and proper shape and size of base. This Scientific Anglers' (3M) System 2, 89 reel reveals some of these features. This model has a disk-drag system.

Rods And Reels

whether from a fresh fish making a run or an angler stripping off line. The drag should never allow spool overrun, and it should exert solid, steady pressure during the fight to land a fish. Drags usually feature either ratchet-and-pawl systems or disks. (Sometimes the two are combined.)

Ratchet-and-pawl drag systems are the most common. They are easy to use and designed to maintain rather light tension when line is reeled in while allowing adjustments for line being taken off the spool. Adjustments depend upon the amount of tension your leader will take, and the drag should always be tested before casting to make sure it is set lower than the tippet's breaking point.

Disk-drag systems use pads which exert pressure directly on the reel spool. They come in several designs and are most common with saltwater reels or in situations where the angler will deal with truly big fish. They can take a lot of pressure without seizing up or burning out, which sometimes happens with ratchet-and-pawl systems that are not designed for maintaining considerable tension over extended periods of time.

Ratchet-and-pawl systems are best for most freshwater species; however, king salmon, steelhead and stripers are exceptions. All but the smallest of saltwater species are better handled on disk-drag systems.

Most reels come with the option of either-hand retrieve, meaning you can switch from right-hand to left-hand reeling easily. To make the switch using a ratchet-and-pawl system, a pawl is removed and flipped over. Some single-action reels have a double-pawl system with only one being activated, depending upon which hand is operating the reel. This is a good feature; however, make sure there are instructions with the reel explaining the retrieve switchover. Many disk-drag systems are also capable of conversion, but it can be complicated. With drags, it is best to make sure that you specify whether you want right-hand or left-hand retrieve when purchasing the reel.

Finally, do not overlook the importance of reel capacity and the shape and size of its base, or "feet." There is nothing more frustrating than a reel seat's sleeves not fitting over the feet of a reel.

Reel capacity, which is the amount of line and backing the spool can hold, is a significant factor. In quality reels, this will be stated in these terms: "To DT7F with 150 yards of backing." Double-tapered lines are the bulkiest; this tells you that the reel in question would hold other line types and a comparable amount of backing quite comfortably. Make sure you check capacity. You want a reel reasonably full—it provides better balance and quicker retrieval as you reel in line. You should not have a reel that balances perfectly with a rod but has inadequate spool capacity.

There are several points to keep in mind when selecting a rod and reel. You need to have a balanced outfit, and both the rod and reel should be suited to your type of fishing. Give careful thought to the various performance factors available in these vital pieces of equipment. The rod and reel are, unquestionably, the two most significant purchases of a fly-fishing outfit.

3

Line Identification
And Selection

Technological advances have revolutionized fly rods as well as fly lines. Silk lines, which required dressing and drying after every outing, used to be the standard for top-level angling equipment. Some of those same lines are now collectors' items.

Today, high-performance lines in various colors and types are available. They can be used for everything from delicate casts with a diminutive 1-weight rod to the weight needed for prodigious casts or sinking ability to get deep beneath the surface quickly. Best of all, not only do these lines perform well but they are virtually maintenance-free.

When choosing a line, keep in mind the function it performs. Standard spinning and casting tackle use the lure's weight to carry the presentation to its intended destination; fly fishing uses the line to perform this task. Indeed, the line is the cast in fly fishing. Different situations and fish species require different lines; however, always match your line to your rod. A balanced outfit makes all the difference in the world—without one, you're in trouble. If you have a fine line and an expensive rod that are badly mismatched, it will feel like you're casting a 30-foot rope with a broom handle!

There are four basic considerations in selecting a fly line: weight (to match your rod), type of taper, color and whether it should float or sink. These considerations may vary, depending upon the type of fishing conditions you will encounter. Wind factors, water depth, fish species and other circumstances must be

Lines come in various weights, tapers and colors. Fly fishermen should base their selection on personal needs. Shown here are double-tapered lines (top row) and weight-forward lines (middle and bottom rows). These lines vary in weight and color.

analyzed in advance. This does not suggest, however, that you need several different lines for every rod.

The fly-fishing beginner can utilize one or two lines for various conditions and fish species. Diversification and specialized lines can wait until the beginner gains experience.

The Importance Of Line Weight

Fly-fishing lines used to be identified by diameter instead of weight. Letters of the alphabet symbolized diameter measurement, resulting in a complex, confusing system. For example, a rod might have required an "H" line. The problem was which H line? Because the lines varied considerably in weight, two lines with the same diameter (hence, the same class) could be appropriate for different types of rods.

Modern line classification is simple and uniform. The American Fishing Tackle Manufacturers Association developed a system that actually weighs the first 30 feet of line in grains. Based on how many grains the line weighs, it is assigned a number. For example, a 4-weight line means the first 30 feet fall in a weight range between 114 and 126 grains (120 grains is the standard); a 9-weight line falls between 230 and 250 grains (240 grains is the standard). Those technicalities do not really matter. The primary concern is knowing the number assigned to a given line. This technique has prevented much frustration for many fisherman.

A line that is one number removed from your rod's number will work. For example, a 4-weight line performs satisfactorily on a 5-weight rod. Some lines are made with two weight classifications, such as WF-4-5-F which denotes a weight-forward, floating line in the 4- or 5-weight category. Generally, most tackle stores have lines in several weights and tapers. Unless you are an advanced fly fisherman with a reason for deviation, you should purchase the same weight as your rod.

Specific rod and line weights fit certain situations, which will be covered in more detail in later chapters. Generally, lines in the 1- to 5-weight class are for small streams, small flies and the smaller fish species; medium weight lines in the 6- to 8-weight classes are best for all-purpose freshwater fishing; and those in the 10-weight or above class are reserved for saltwater fishing and maybe one or two special freshwater situations, such as those presented by king salmon or striped bass.

Basic Fly Line Shapes

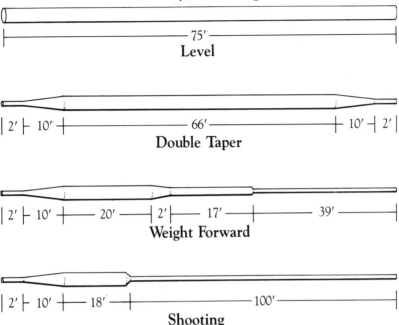

|——————————————— 75' ———————————————|
Level

| 2' |— 10" —|———————————————— 66' ————————————————|— 10' —| 2' |
Double Taper

| 2' |— 10' —|——— 20' ———|— 2' |——— 17' ———|——————— 39' ———————|
Weight Forward

| 2' |— 10' —|——— 18' ———|———————————— 100' ————————————|
Shooting

Double-tapered line is easy to mend on the water because of its uniform construction and reduced surface tension. Also, an angler can use the other end when the first end wears out. Weight-forward line casts farther because of its reduced line diameter following the thicker front section. The shooting head is a refinement of the weight-forward line.

Types Of Tapers

Along with line weight, you will need to determine the type of taper you need. Level lines are the least expensive and have the same diameter from one end to the other. They cost less because they are easy to make. Level lines are acceptable for panfishing and fly fishing for trout in small, swift streams where neither distance nor delicacy matter; however, even the beginning angler can make a better choice.

Double-tapered line is probably the best choice for the fly-fishing beginner. Double tapers are not quite as popular as they were a decade ago—they used to be considered the all-around fishing line. Manufacturers probably realized that a properly maintained double-tapered line lasts twice as long as any other type of taper because only one end is used. Normally, only the first 50 or

60 feet of line are used (lines are usually 75, 90 or 100 feet in length). The 30-foot actual taper at the line's opposite end remains almost new. When the terminal end becomes worn, reverse the line.

The double-tapered line works great for false casting, roll casting and delicately presenting a fly. In short, the double-tapered line is an excellent choice for the beginner.

In the last decade or so, weight-forward lines have become more popular than double-tapered lines. Weight-forward lines put a lot of line weight into the first 30 feet of the line, thus the term *weight-forward*. Those initial 30 feet are trailed by line much smaller in diameter. The momentum of the first 30 feet pulls this trailing line along rapidly. This enables the angler to shoot a lot of line and get longer casts without extra effort.

There is a major drawback to the weight-forward line. If you use more than 30 feet of line to false cast, the cast will fall apart. The smaller line diameter cannot support the heavy head in the air. Weight-forward lines cannot be reversed; once the casting end wears out, it's time to buy a new line.

In addition to the standard weight-forward line, there are numerous special-purpose lines that function similarly—concentrating weight in the front portion of the line. These include the bass bug taper, saltwater taper and the triangle taper that Lee Wulff introduced a few years before his death. These lines are beneficial in strong winds or when making long casts. They are not, however, good for "delicate" situations.

Another line, the shooting head, is a variation on the weight-forward line. The taper is the same but there is no running line. This means you can put more line in the air without your cast breaking down. The shooting head or shooting taper is a line designed for exceptionally long casts, such as when steelhead or salmon fishing on big rivers. Sometimes, a length of monofilament appears before the backing, allowing the entire line to be "shot." ("Shooting" line is covered in Chapter 7.)

Line Color

Anglers have an ample selection of line colors to choose from. Bright, high-visibility lines are popular, and they have some real advantages. For one thing, lines in colors such as bright yellow or fluorescent orange are easily seen. This enables the angler to follow the progress of a tiny fly or readily note a twitch or stop. It also permits anglers to analyze their casts. Bright lines are a photographer's delight. When you see a color photograph of a fly fisherman in action, he will most likely be using a high-visibility line.

On the other hand, some anglers believe that fish see the lines, too. This may be true, especially with sinking or sink-tip lines. Many veteran fly fishermen prefer somber tones for their fly lines. Good selections include brown, gray, dull green and off-white.

Line Function

When fly lines land on the water, they either float or sink. There are many variations of sinking lines, including those with lead core, which make their way toward the bottom rapidly; those which both float and sink (the sink-tip lines mentioned earlier); and those which stay on the surface when dressed and sink gently when untreated.

Technology has given us floating lines that require no dressing or special treatment—just an occasional cleaning. Most floating lines have a special coating that traps air within the line and keeps it riding high in the water.

Floating lines are used for several types of fly fishing. They work best with dry flies and surface bugs or poppers, as well as nymphs. Floating lines also work with streamers in shallow water, as well as water with moderate current.

Sinking lines come in different sinking speeds. In a powerful river with an average depth of several feet, a lead-core line with a rapid sink rate may be best; a slow-flowing river of the same depth would need a sinking line with moderate sinking speed. The sinking speed should coincide with the conditions.

Line Terminology

Line weight is indicated by a simple numbering system. It runs from 1 to 15—just like rod weights. Once you select a rod, its weight tells you the required line weight. The three most common descriptions of taper are L (level), DT (double-tapered) and WF (weight-forward). Additional lettering or descriptions indicating bug taper, shooting head and long belly may also be present. Similarly, letters are used to let the angler know whether the line is a floating, sinking or float/sink line. After everything is com-

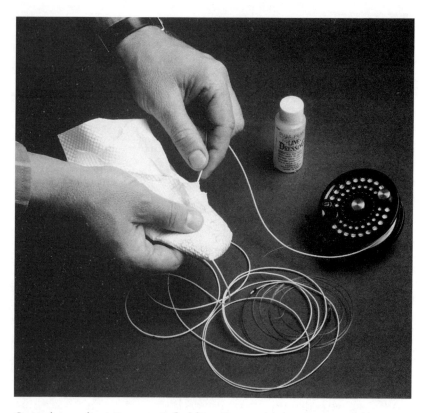

Caring for your line is important in fly fishing. Commercial cleansers are available at most fishing-tackle stores. Mild soap and a soft cloth will also do the job. Modern fly lines require no care beyond cleaning.

bined, a direct, simple "code" for line descriptions results. For example, DT-5-F represents a double-tapered, floating line for a 5-weight rod; WF-13-S indicates a weight-forward, sinking line for a 13-weight rod. The DT-5-F would be a good line for trout fishing or panfishing. The WF-13-S works great when fishing for tarpon or other big saltwater species.

There are a lot of good fly lines on the market. Quality lines are not cheap; you usually pay for performance.

Line Care

Line care is a simple process. Occasional cleaning with mild soap and a wet cloth enhances performance. Avoid letting the line come in contact with solvents, such as suntan lotions and bug sprays. Casting without a leader can cause fraying, and pinching the line between the reel and frame can crack or damage the coating. Make sure you do not store lines for lengthy periods of time in damp, musty places or hot places, such as direct sunlight or the trunk of a car. Check your rod guides for rough spots once or twice during the season. If you notice abrasions on the line (as opposed to cracks in the coating which tell you it is time for a new one), sharp edges on guides are usually the culprit.

With minimal care, a fine double-tapered line can last for several seasons. Finally, better lines mean better casting performance. In other words, if you want to be a great fly fisherman, a good line is just as important as a good rod.

4

Leaders And Tippets

Terminal tackle for the fly fisherman is appropriately called a leader. This slender piece of nylon monofilament is literally the "leading" element of the cast. Sometimes, the leader is "tipped" or completed with a short strand of material, the tippet. Leaders vary considerably in length and strength according to the type of fishing; however, the leader's basic purpose remains the same—no matter what the species or conditions.

As mentioned in the preceding chapter, line weight—not lure weight—gives the angler distance in fly fishing. The line, therefore, needs to have appreciable weight and bulk, yet delicacy of presentation. Presenting a fly with a virtually invisible leader so that it flutters to the surface like a gently falling leaf is no small part of this angling technique.

Leader Material And Terminology

Many materials have been used to manufacture leaders. These have included horsehair, silkworm secretions, catgut and a host of similar natural materials. A small diameter, comparative invisibility and strength have always been key criteria for leaders. Today, virtually all fly-fishing leader material is nylon monofilament or some other related synthetic. These materials have improved dramatically in recent years. The basic trend with this particular technology has been moving toward greater leader strength in relation to diameter.

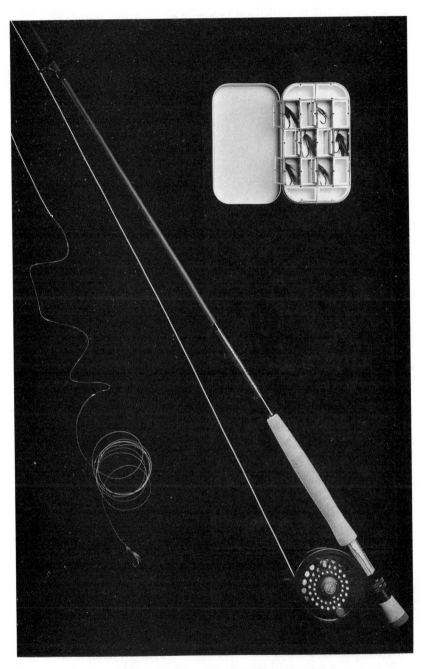

Leaders are an important part of fly fishing's terminal-tackle setup. Whether they are knotted (shown here) or knotless, leaders play an essential role in making the presentation realistic.

Leaders And Tippets

Diameter is one of the more complicated areas of fly fishing. Rather than referring to leaders as fishing line with tapered 2-pound test at the end, established practice describes leaders in categories of diameter. When a beginner hears someone mention "a 10-foot leader tapering to 7X" or "use of 5X tippets," it can be confusing. The "X factor" describes diameter with categories ranging from 0X to 8X. Each change represents a variation in diameter of $1/1000$ of an inch; the larger the X number, the smaller the diameter (see corresponding chart on next page).

One simple way to learn and remember corresponding leader diameters for X factors is to determine the diameter that "X" should be and subtract it from the number 11. For example, 5X would be .006 inch.

Although the diameter is undeniably significant, two other factors are even more critical. They are leader suppleness, or flexibility, and leader strength. Many anglers, particularly fly-fishing newcomers, think in terms of line strength rather than diameter: the lower the breaking point, the smaller the diameter. Because leader material has improved in recent years, old formulas, such as those maintaining that a 7X leader tested at one pound, are no longer valid.

Technology has also increased the flexibility of material in higher X categories. It's possible to use stronger leaders while getting casts to turn over well and avoid drag. Drag, which can be described as a fly unnaturally moving or pulling through the water at a speed that is different from the current's, will repel more fish than a large diameter line.

Types Of Leaders

There are two basic leader categories: knotted and knotless. Both taper down from a thick section of monofilament where the leader and line join to a much smaller diameter at the monofilament's end where the fly attaches. The leader's butt section (the end where it joins the line) should be fairly close to the line's size. It should also be stiffer than the final or tippet section. This permits smoother turnover in casting, meaning the fly will be the last thing to touch the water. Leaders, therefore, perform better when they have a smooth "taper." There are some special situations, such as fishing for bedding bream, when a "flat" or untapered leader will work; however, it will not handle well on the cast.

X Factor Or Designation	Leader Diameter
8X	.003 inch
7X	.004 inch
6X	.005 inch
5X	.006 inch
4X	.007 inch
3X	.008 inch
2X	.009 inch
1X	.010 inch
0X	.011 inch

This chart describes leader diameters using X factors, ranging from 0 to 8. Each category changes by 1/1000 of an inch. The larger the X factor, the smaller the diameter.

Single Strand Or Knotless Leaders

Another decision fly-fishing anglers must make is whether to use knotted segments of leader with descending sizes and carefully selected lengths or a knotless leader which, thanks to modern technology, goes from butt section down to its end with the same amount of taper. At first glance, the latter would seem distinctly preferable, and it is almost the only option available for those who buy ready-to-use leaders.

Single-strand leaders normally come in three lengths: 7½, 9 or 12 feet. Twelve-foot leaders are often difficult to find—even in sporting goods stores specializing in fly-fishing equipment. Another problem with knotless leaders is that you must add tippets to them or they will not last long. After changing flies about six times, you find yourself too far up the taper.

Even though there are some disadvantages, most fly fishermen use knotless leaders. They are unquestionably more convenient, giving anglers more time to actually fish when on the water. Knotless leaders are the best choice for beginning fly fishermen.

Knotted Leaders

Knotted leaders save money. You can buy several spools of good leader material in varying sizes, achieve solid mastery of the blood knot (see Chapter 8) and produce your own leaders. For the same amount of money, you can either purchase six knotless leaders or material to produce 75 to 100 knotted leaders. Aside from the necessary nylon spools, your only investment is time.

Another distinct advantage to tying your own leaders is the ability to make them precisely as long and strong as you want. This is particularly important in situations where a lengthy leader is desirable, such as when fishing heavily pressured trout in slow-moving streams, on creeks with tricky cross currents or in small lakes. For saltwater fly fishing, it is almost essential to tie your own leaders.

Preparing knotted leaders is a comparatively simple process after mastering the blood knot and developing "formulas" for the proper material lengths for each section. The trial-and-error process should help find what leader lengths and section combinations work best for you.

In creating leaders, some general guidelines exist. First, you need to know the requirements a leader must have in order to perform well. It must be tied so the power of the cast progresses smoothly from the line into the leader. This will cause it to turn the fly over and set it down gently. If the leader is poorly proportioned, it will most likely collapse at the end of the cast, piling up on the surface.

To achieve this "turn-over" effect, the leader should have strands of decreasing length from the butt downward. This resembles the precise taper of a knotless leader. It also simplifies the actual process of tying.

The butt section's diameter is the key factor in the castability of both knotted and knotless leaders. It needs to be fairly close to the size of the line (two-thirds to three-fourths of the line's diameter) to perform well. If the butt section's monofilament is exceptionally stiff, you may not need as much diameter. You should link

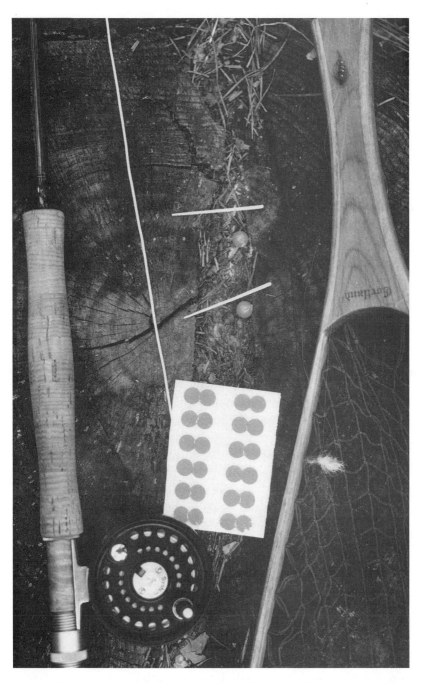

Bright strike indicators attached to leaders can be a real asset. Several types of strike indicators can be used for various fish species.

Leaders And Tippets

the leader and line with a nail knot and take 4 or 5 inches of each in your hand. With equal portions of line and leader in hand, make a "U" with the knot in the middle. If this is done easily, you have a good match between line and leader butt in terms of diameter and flexibility. If the "U" does not form nicely, the butt section may be too stiff or not stiff enough.

The next section of a knotted leader is the taper, although this terminology is a bit misleading. (The leader really tapers in diameter throughout its length as each new section of monofilament is added.) In the middle or taper section of knotted leaders, the monofilament strands get shorter—even as the rate of taper increases. You can manipulate this leader section quite a bit to get different performances. The shorter these middle strands, the faster the casting power moves to the tippet; the longer the strands, the slower the process. If you have trouble turning the tippet over, shorten the sections. Ideally, you should tie a leader that barely turns the tippet over on a normal cast. You want the fly to ease down to the surface like a parachutist floating gently to the earth's surface.

The third and final section of tapered leaders is the tippet. This is a single strand of monofilament with the least amount of strength. The tippet should always be longer than the leader's taper strands which immediately precede it; however, many factors need to be considered before a decision is made on tippet length.

The longer the tippet, the less the casting control. This is especially true when fishing in the wind or working with bulky flies, which create a lot of air-resistance. "Wind knots" are common when your tippet is too long or when fishing in these adverse conditions; however, they really come from a breakdown in the continuity of the cast. When this happens, shorten the tippet. A wind knot (a simple overhand or "hard" knot) decreases line strength by about 50 percent.

On the other hand, a long tippet is more flexible than a short one. This results in better drifting situations when you are fishing in currents. The little curves that form when a fly gently lies on the water help avoid drag. When fishing with a 1- or 2-pound-test tippet, it should be fairly long to provide some "give." This enables it to absorb some of the shock during the hookset.

There is a long-established formula—often called the 60-20-

Make Your Own 12-Foot Knotted Leaders

	Leader 1	Leader 2	Leader 3
	36" - 25-lb. test	36" - 25-lb. test	28" - 25-lb. test
Butt	24" - 20-lb. test	24" - 20-lb. test	18" - 20-lb. test
	16" - 15-lb. test	20" - 15-lb. test	16" - 15-lb. test
	12" - 10-lb. test	12" - 10-lb. test	14" - 10-lb. test
	10" - 08-lb. test	12" - 08-lb. test	12" - 08-lb. test
Taper	7" - 06-lb. test	12" - 06-lb. test	8" - 06-lb. test
	7" - 04-lb. test		8" - 04-lb. test
			8" - 02-lb. test
Tippet	32" - 02-lb. test	28" - 04-lb. test	36" - 01-lb. test

This chart shows three different 12-foot leaders you can tie. The 60-20-20 rule applies for all three examples: 60 percent, butt section; 20 percent, middle section; and 20 percent, tippet. Leader 2 has the most practical tippet size.

20 rule—for linking the three portions of a knotted leader (butt, taper and tippet). The formula provides a useful general guide on how to form a knotted leader. The figures mean that 60 percent of the leader's length should be in the butt, 20 percent in the taper section and 20 percent in the tippet.

The most practical tippet length is the 28-inch, 4-pound test material. It takes a proficient, powerful caster to handle the longer, more delicate tippets suggested in the other two examples. You will also notice that each of the sample leaders corresponds roughly to the 60-20-20 guidelines.

In the final analysis, your leader choice will depend upon your casting abilities, the fish species, prevailing conditions (such as wind or water clarity) and other factors.

5

How To Fish Flies

Fishing with flies immediately implies fishing with insect-imitating lures. To some degree, this is true; however, several "flies" imitate non-insect food items, such as minnows, crayfish, crabs, other crustaceans, lizards, worms and frogs. In essence, the sky is the limit when it comes to fly patterns. The energy and ingenuity of anglers who tie flies are the only limiting factors in the development of new patterns. Understanding the types of flies and their intended purposes will help fly fishermen fool some of the fish at least some of the time.

There are basically two categories of flies: attractors and imitators. One attracts the attention of fish, even though it may not look like a specific food item; the other is an artful imitation of the real thing.

Attractors

Although attractor flies may not imitate specific insects or food items, they sometimes resemble several things that fish eat. The Royal Wulff (named after its creator, Lee Wulff—one of the great names in American fly fishing), for example, looks like no single insect but has the general shape of many insects popular in the trout diet. This pattern is probably the world's single most popular dry fly. Wulff believed the fly's shape attracted the fish. The Royal Wulff's showy, white hair wings and flashy red body also attract fishermen. The fly always looks good in the water which builds angler confidence. The same can be said of many

Shown here are some popular fly patterns. The top row includes a crayfish imitator (left) and frog imitator (right); second row has a Clouser Minnow (left), Scud (middle) and grasshopper (right) pattern; third row includes a dragonfly imitator (left) and a Sea Ducer attractor pattern (right); a lizard/snake/worm/eel imitator stands alone in the bottom row.

streamers, especially the brilliantly colored ones like the Black-Nosed Dace: Their hue catches the eyes of fishermen but their alluring, minnow-like shape draws strikes from fish.

Indeed, *shape* is the operative word for most attractors. The pattern enters the fish's vision window and, because it has the general configuration of things the fish is accustomed to eating, triggers a strike. Sound and motion can also be factors in drawing strikes. Popping bugs, which are popular bass lures, make a distinctive sound when retrieved with a sharp jerk. They attract fish with sound instead of appearance. Another way to attract fish is to make your dry fly "dance," or impart movement. This resembles a struggling insect.

Mark Cathey, a legendary fisherman from the Great Smoky Mountains of North Carolina, earned considerable local renown for his "dance of the dry fly" in the 1920s and 1930s. At times, he would make his fly dash and dart on the surface of a single pool for 10 to 15 minutes!

When there seems to be little fish-feeding activity, attractors may work the best; repeated pattern offerings may eventually provoke a strike. Dry flies are easily visible. In tumbling, fast-moving freestone streams, buoyant, high-riding attractor patterns are easy to follow. This is also true when fishing in conditions of low or poor light, such as at dawn, dusk or during overcast, foggy days.

Imitators

The combination of a growing awareness of entomology and fish biology, ever-increasing numbers of innovative fly-tiers and the availability of a wide range of tying materials means that patterns are available (or can be created) to imitate almost anything. These range from the tiniest midge patterns tied on minute hooks, such as No. 24 and 26 (or even smaller), to huge flies several inches in length requiring powerful rods and perfect timing during the cast. Even though there is a wide variety of imitators, they can be viewed from a simpler perspective which categorizes them according to where and how they are fished. Generally, flies are fished in two places: on the surface and underwater. Subsurface flies can be fished in various locations, such as along the bottom, in the film at or just beneath the surface or somewhere in between. It is easier, however, to categorize flies into two basic classes: surface and subsurface.

The Royal Wulff is probably the most popular dry-fly pattern in all of fly fishing. It is actually an attractor pattern that resembles several insects in a trout's diet.

Surface Flies

Most popular gamefish get 90 percent or more of their food from beneath the surface. Even trout, which are famous for surface-feeding, obtain most of their sustenance from underwater.

Most fly fishermen spend too much time working the surface. If 90 percent of a fish's diet comes from beneath the surface, logic would dictate that 90 percent of fishing efforts should focus on that area. Given this consideration, the obvious question is, "Why is so much emphasis placed on surface fly fishing?"

One reason surface flies appeal to anglers is because they are visible. It's thrilling to see a trophy rainbow inhale a dry fly or watch an aggressive largemouth bass explode on a popping bug. That thrill—watching the strike—causes anglers to continue fishing dries, even though other flies could produce more action.

There is also the myth that true sportsmen use only surface flies. Englishman Frederick Halford, the progenitor of dry-fly fishing, was the originator of this belief. Later, a similar attitude prevailed among many members of the "Catskill school"—an Eastern elite in fly fishing's American history. Anglers should savor the thrills of surface fly fishing; however, they should not deny themselves the pleasure of trying other rewarding approaches.

Dry flies can be an asset for the fly-fishing beginner; the angler "sees" the surface strike when it occurs. This makes hooksetting easier. Delicate hits on subsurface flies, especially nymphs, are often difficult to detect. Distinguishing between an actual strike and the fly bumping against rocks is another problem that anglers frequently encounter with subsurface flies. In moving water, surface flies show the novice "drag" and how to avoid it.

Dry Flies. Mentioning dry flies normally evokes thoughts of trout and salmon. Yet many other species, ranging from panfish to voracious pike in freshwater to several saltwater gamefish, can be caught with dries. Whatever fish species is involved, a key factor in dry-fly fishing is the fish's "window of vision," or what the fish sees when it looks toward the surface.

The window is like a cone: The fish sees objects in the heart of the window clearly while objects on the edge are blurry, and the deeper the fish, the wider the window. Fish that feed on top are usually suspended near the surface; their window tends to be small.

The way that fish perceive insect imitations on the surface determines whether or not they will strike. Fly-tiers constantly debate about fly designs relating to underwater vision. Two things are always in this debate: A dry fly must be visible to a fish for it to strike; a dry fly must look like something edible to elicit a take.

This leads to the two basic types of dry-fly fishing: casting to visible fish and to invisible ones. When casting to visible fish, anglers usually see a rise or series of rises and then cast a fly to that same place. Casting to invisible fish is in reality "blind casting." The fisherman works spots that seem like promising locations or have proven productive in the past. This is an excellent tactic for trout in freestone streams, especially those not rich with insect life. Under these conditions, trout do most of their feeding opportunistically instead of zeroing in on hatches. This approach also works well for panfish, bass and many other freshwater species. It is less useful in saltwater.

When fishing surface flies, anglers have the advantage of seeing the fish when it strikes. This summer steelhead took a dry fly near the surface, giving the angler a visual treat.

Window Of Vision

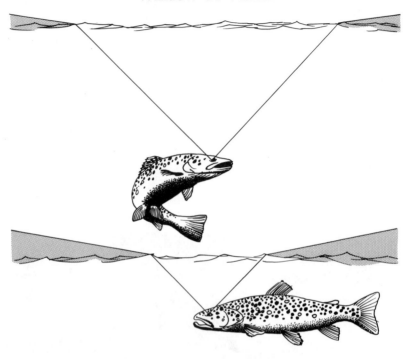

The fish's window of vision has always been a phenomenon. The window is an angle with a constant vertex (the fish's eye). As the fish nears the surface, the window becomes smaller. The fish sees everything within the window so anglers need to be cautious.

Effective blind casting requires that anglers cover a lot of water. However, there are some exceptions: Occasionally, you have a limited stretch of water assigned to you, such as a beat; you happen to be in a "honey hole" which holds plenty of fish; or you know a trophy fish is in a particular place. In these circumstances, you should change patterns frequently. When you find a dry fly that draws consistent strikes, stick with it. If certain types of pools or holding spots produce hits, give those locations special attention. Sometimes, a fly cast repeatedly to a specific spot will eventually evoke a strike. Fish may think a hatch is occurring and will begin eating, or they just might become irritated.

When you see several fish rising in a single pool or area, they usually are feeding on a particular hatching insect. This presents the opportunity to cast to feeding fish. It is often necessary to match the hatch accurately. Keep experimenting until you find what it takes to pique the interest of the fish. Sometimes it is helpful to catch and examine one of the insects the fish are eating. Most accomplished dry-fly fishermen are first-rate amateur entomologists—some even carry compact fly-tying kits.

Occasionally, a multiple hatch (more than one type of insect emerging) occurs, presenting additional problems. For example, you may match one insect exactly only to discover that it's not what the fish are eating. When fish are feeding voraciously during a heavy hatch, change flies until you find something that works. This is no time to stick with an old favorite just because it has taken a lot of fish in the past.

Sometimes "fishing the rise" will involve a single fish. Then a double problem presents itself: The angler must offer a fly that the

Catching fish often depends upon matching the hatch correctly. Experimenting is a key to finding the best imitator of the hatching insect. (Here, the white specks in the air are hatching insects.)

fish will take, and the fly must be cast in a way that does not spook the fish.

Poppers, Sliders And Other Bugs. Bugs are a popular food item for bass, panfish, northern pike, redfish, jack crevalle and many other species. Bugs come in various sizes and shapes. Many are tied or constructed with a concave face. This causes them to create a bubble of water when retrieved. If worked vigorously, they make a distinct "popping" sound, giving them their name. Bugs with a broad, flat surface can also be rapidly retrieved with somewhat similar, albeit not as loud, sound effects. Another bug category is sliders. They have rounded heads enabling them to move easily and quietly through the water.

Many surface patterns described as "bugs" are neither poppers nor sliders. They are commonly made of soft material, such as deer or elk hair; however, tiny cork creations used for panfish also fall into this category.

Most bugging is done in still water, and controlling slack is crucial for success. This is done by handling the retrieve with the "off," or non-casting, hand and keeping the rodtip low and parallel to the water.

Bugs, especially the large ones used for bass and saltwater fishing, are difficult to cast. They are heavy and air-resistant. Rods used for casting bugs are usually 7-weight or higher; longer rods, as well as shorter leaders, are a plus. Fortunately, finesse is seldom a factor when fishing bugs. Fishermen can execute sloppy or splashy casts and still produce results. When fishing bugs in freshwater situations, long-distance casts are seldom necessary.

From the coastal regions to the vast expansions of the American heartland, fishermen are utilizing the bug-fishing technique. It is one of the easiest fly-fishing methods to pursue and many fish species can be readily taken.

Subsurface Flies

When fishing subsurface flies, the action occurs out of sight so the sport takes on a different dimension. Touch, instinct and experience play prominent roles in this method.

Wet Flies. Although not used as frequently today, wet flies are the oldest of all artificials. Before the late 19th century, the vast majority of fly fishermen depended upon wet flies. The advent of dry flies pushed wet flies from center stage—even today anglers

Poppers, sliders and other bugs are popular in fly fishing. Some patterns that are widely used include cork poppers (top left), deer-hair sliders (top right), foam divers (bottom left) and deer-hair bass bugs (bottom right).

fishing beneath the surface opt for streamers or nymphs. Wet flies, however, still work ... and well. Every fly fisherman should know how to use them.

Wet flies come in two basic styles: (1) some soft hackle wrapped around the top part of the hook shank, which is also covered with some sort of material and (2) a wing stretching back over the top of the hook shank, which is referred to as a downwing fly. Wet flies, like dries, are categorized as either attractors or imitators. The attractors are flashy flies with bright colors or tinsel. Some examples are the Parmachene Belle and Royal Coachman, which are old favorites for trout, and many of the best-known salmon patterns. (Tinsel-laden patterns have become prominent in saltwater fishing.)

Wet-fly imitators do not duplicate specific insects as well as their dry-fly counterparts. They are tied with drab-colored materials, giving a vague impression of something natural. Wet flies are frequently fished in tandem with a dull imitator used as a dropper behind an attractor. Most strikes occur on the imitator when tandem rigs are used; however, anglers believe it is the bright pattern that grabs the fish's attention.

How To Fish Flies

Wet flies can be fished in several ways. This includes upstream with a dead drift toward the angler, across the current with mending to avoid drag (see Chapter 7) and downstream casts with the drift away from the angler. Retrieval methods commonly used are the straight strip, hand-twist and finger-twist.

These retrieves, which are also used with streamers, give motion to the wet fly while providing line control. The index or middle finger of the rod hand controls the line while the other hand makes the retrieve. The strip retrieve involves casting the wet fly then working it back with a series of pulling motions, pausing in between. The length and speed of the strip, along with the timing of the pause, can be varied according to what the fish prefer. This flexibility in technique is important.

Both hand-twist and finger-twist retrieves involve steady, repetitive motion from the time they begin until the time the fly is lifted from the water for another cast. Any time the fly stops or meets resistance, set the hook. When wet-fly fishing you need to watch the line. A sudden twitch or other unnatural movement may indicate a strike.

Streamers. The majority of streamers imitate minnows, although there are a few eel and lizard patterns. It is also commonplace, especially among old-timers, to refer to streamers tied with animal hair as bucktails. (The term *streamer* is reserved for patterns using feathers in the tying process.) All flies of this type have a streamlined profile comparable to that of a minnow, and most patterns are tied on long-shank hooks. In a sense, streamers are nothing more than long, large wet flies.

The most common technique for fishing streamers in moving water is to cast them down and across the current. The angler allows the current to sweep the belly of the line, which pulls the fly toward the tail of the pool or run. The retrieving techniques, discussed above, supply the motion during the sweep, working the streamer back upstream. Most strikes occur when the fly straightens out at the end of the sweep, although they may occur at any point during the drift and retrieve. Fish will frequently hook themselves, requiring nothing more than a quick lift of the rodtip for the hookset. In still water, of course, retrieving is just about the only way to create "action." One advantage of streamer fishing is that strikes are easily detected. When fish hit streamers, they do so with a vengeance!

Subsurface fly fishing calls for wet flies and streamers. Some popular wet flies include the Royal Coachman (left) and Red Fox Squirrel Nymph (right), top row; Purple Peril, second row; Caddis Pupa (left) and Black Gnat (right), third row. Popular streamer patterns include Wool Head Sculpin (left) and Muddler Minnow, fourth row; Deer Hair Head Sculpin, fifth row; and Mickey Finn (left) and Spruce Matuka (right), bottom row.

How To Fish Flies   61

Although streamer strikes are easily discerned, placing the fly where it should be is not so simple. A major problem facing streamer fishermen is getting and keeping the fly at the proper depth. Most of the time the streamer should be on or near bottom—a streamer literally bouncing along bottom while being retrieved is ideal. This can be achieved in several ways.

In moving or still waters with some amount of depth, a sinking or sink-tip line is needed. Split shot on the leader a foot or so above the fly can also help, although casting can be more difficult. To get the streamer down fast, many patterns are tied with split-shot "eyes" on the fly or lead strips are wrapped around the hook shank. In particularly fast and deep waters, it is sometimes necessary to use lead-core line in your rig. Materials that absorb water or commercial preparations that speed up the saturation process can be helpful.

The more weight you add, the more difficult it will be to cast. At some point, no matter how well you handle a fly rod, you are going to give yourself a solid thump in the back or head with weighted streamers. Once you reach this "chuck and duck" point, you can either slow down your cast (this prevents your loop from tightening and brings the streamer forward on a higher plane) or use roll casts.

You should match your streamers to the minnows found in the water you're fishing. Muddler Minnows, as well as various colors of Matukas and Shenk Sculpins, work almost anywhere. When standard patterns don't produce strikes, try a streamer tied with rabbit fur. Sometimes these streamers will draw powerful strikes.

Nymphs. Day in and day out, an accomplished nymph fisherman will outfish comparably skilled anglers who use dry flies, wet flies or streamers. This reveals that fish eat an extraordinary amount of nymphs; however, it can be devilishly difficult to become a first-rate nympher. Most aspects of fly fishing are easy to learn, but you can throw simplicity out the window when it comes to nymph fishing. Nymphing is the fly fisherman's consummate challenge. Most nymph masters are devoted anglers who have worked countless hours on the water for many years to achieve their expertise.

The most demanding aspect of fishing nymphs is learning to detect strikes. They come in several forms. A common strike indicator is a tiny float that is usually painted bright orange; it works much like a bobber in the cane-pole days. When the float stops, suddenly moves sideways or darts beneath the surface, you most likely have a strike. It's time to set the hook!

Other strike indicators include small, brightly colored foam patches with adhesive sides that clamp around your leader at the chosen spot, small pieces of high-visibility thread that attach to the leader and some fluorescent coloring where the leader and line join. If you use a dry fly and nymph rig in tandem, the dry fly works as the indicator. (In fast-moving water, use one that rides high, such as a Parachute Adams or a Thunderhead.)

Methods for working nymphs in the water are similar to those already mentioned for other subsurface flies. However, nymphs require special attention to line slack. Always keep the line as tight as possible—without giving the nymph too much action. Using short lines may also be advantageous; the more line you have out, the more likely you will fail in detecting strikes.

Even though nymphing can be frustrating, it has special rewards. You can take fish on nymphs when nothing else works. Nymphing is particularly effective in cold weather when there is no food on the surface and the fishes' slowed metabolisms have left them reluctant to tackle fast-moving flies. Finally, you cannot claim to be a Renaissance fly fisherman, a true angler for all seasons, until you achieve competence with the nymph.

6

Accessories: Essential And Otherwise

Gimmicks and gadgets draw fly fishermen like heavy caddis hatches draw trout. The beginning fly fisherman will most likely be overwhelmed by the wide array of equipment available. Differentiating between what you really need to function effectively as a fly fisherman, what is useful but not mandatory and what is pure luxury is not a simple task.

Fly-fishing accessories will depend upon the fly-fishing technique and situation. A vest is needed when fishing remote free-stone streams; however, it may be an uncomfortable luxury in a boat being poled through the flats in search of bonefish. A creel is convenient when planning to keep fish for dinner; it is not needed when practicing catch-and-release. In other words, the fly fisherman should examine his situation, acquire the basics and select other items in a practical and proficient manner.

Essential Accessories

Clothing. Wading gear will be discussed in Chapter 10. In addition to boots and waders, the fly fisherman should consider other items of clothing. The sport's increasing popularity has been greeted with all sorts of "designer" wear, which manufacturers claim as vital for success. Some clothing items are essential; however, most are luxuries and do nothing to improve your effectiveness in catching fish. In fact, some of the brightly colored outerwear may do the opposite—it may spook the fish.

Many fish species accustomed to clear water do not like flashy

This angler is wearing earth-toned clothing to blend into the background. The art of camou-flage should be learned and used in fly fishing.

Accessories: Essential And Otherwise

Hats with sizeable front bills and neck protection are useful. They protect anglers from the hot sun, offer a shield in windy conditions and aid vision on bright days.

colors. Earth tones—browns and greens—are generally preferable to pastels. Beyond that, common sense and comfort are the main determinants in clothing selection. Generally, clothing items you already own will suffice.

Most anglers will purchase a cap or hat. These come in various designs created specifically for the fisherman. If you plan to fish in windy conditions, such as when fishing Western trout streams, a hat with a "stampede string" or a loop that hooks to the back of your vest may save you some hatless grief. You will also want headwear that shields your eyes, head and neck from the sun. A "flats hat" (actually a cap), which has a front and back brim, provides this type of protection.

Protection For Rods And Reels. Most rods come with a cloth sleeve and an aluminum or plastic tube. Reels, however, seldom come with a protective container, although some expensive models include fitted cases or chamois cases lined with fleece. You may want to consider purchasing a rod case—made of cloth or expandable plastic—if you travel a lot.

Diary. A diary may seem strange to list under essential equipment, but it is an extremely important learning tool. Recording your fishing experiences will give you insight on how fish act in various wind, precipitation and temperature conditions. Fly fish-

Sample Diary Page

Today's Date:	*June 10, 19xx*
Place:	*AuSable River (MI)*
Approach:	*Wading (Hip Boots)*
Weather:	*Warm and windless*
Water Temp:	*60 degrees*
Hatches:	*Mayfly*
Effective Flies:	*No. 8 Irresistible*
Fish caught:	*Brown trout (4 lbs.)*
Location of Fish:	*Behind rock in eddy*
Comments:	*Switched from nymphing*

Diaries are readily available for the fly fisherman, but you can easily create your own. Here are some categorical topics you may want to include in your diary. Make sure to leave space on each page for diagrams and drawings.

ing is a lifelong exercise in education; a diary provides invaluable information.

Fly Boxes. Storage boxes for flies come in many shapes and sizes. They range in cost from nothing to $100. Sometimes fly boxes or containers are necessary; you cannot stick six flies in your hat band or on your vest fleece patch.

Fly boxes hold flies without damaging them, and they permit the angler to arrange them in an orderly fashion. This enables the angler to immediately find a certain pattern when a sudden hatch occurs. Fly boxes need good air circulation. If fishing in windy conditions, you should have fly boxes that have clips for holding individual hooks. This prevents a sudden gust of wind from blowing a batch of flies away.

You can utilize containers that cost nothing. For example,

clear containers that hold film are excellent "boxes" for small flies or poppers. Small, plastic medicine bottles and boxes also work well. These types of boxes, however, offer little air circulation and will most likely break easily. A better choice, in the long run, is to acquire boxes made specifically for flies.

These boxes fall into several categories: simple plastic, metal, those with foam inserts, those with clips and those with compartments. There are also books or wallets available with several "pages" of fleece material to hold flies. Some saltwater fly fishermen have large wooden boxes specifically designed to hold numerous flies already attached to shock tippets.

When comparing metal boxes and plastic boxes, you need to weigh the higher price of aluminum against the fragility of plastic. If you tumble on some rocks with plastic boxes in your vest, you will most likely have some broken plastic boxes. Metal boxes often have air holes, making rust less of a problem. The joints on plastic boxes wear out with repeated usage. Finally, some plastic boxes will interact negatively with certain materials, such as glue and fly flotant.

If you want to hold individual flies or small groups of flies in place, there are several options. Boxes with magnetic strips work well for small flies (size 12 or smaller); however, you can lose some carrying capacity.

Boxes with springs or clips hold flies safely and securely, but they can be a major nuisance. The clips are sometimes stubborn when inserting or releasing a fly; you frequently dull hook points. Clips may also contain hidden moisture that causes hooks to deteriorate. Some other types of boxes have foam-lined interiors. Evenly spaced ridges provide places to insert hook points. Repeated use, however, will eventually cause the foam to tear. Some companies manufacture replacement liners.

Finally, the most expensive boxes have individual compartments with spring lids. There is no wasted space, and the abundance of compartments makes it possible to segregate 15 to 20 patterns within a single box. If the box slips or flips while in use, the only flies that will fall out are those in the compartments without the lids secure. These are the best boxes available, and most affluent anglers use them.

The Landing Net. There are at least two reasons why landing nets are essential: (1) Your chances of losing a trophy fish will

A landing net greatly simplifies things. It decreases your chances of losing fish and helps in releasing fish unharmed.

decrease and (2) it's easy to release netted fish unharmed.

Wading fishermen can decide between collapsible nets and nets with fixed or rigid frames; fishermen usually rely on larger nets with 3- to 4-foot handles. The collapsible net is handy because you can remove it from its holster with one hand when needed. (It stays out of the way the rest of the time.) However, this type of net cannot be used with chest waders; its holster is usually attached to the angler's belt.

Fixed framed nets usually come with an elastic strap attached. This enables the fisherman to extend the net to the desired location, landing the fish. Unfortunately, these nets have a nasty habit of becoming entangled in bushes and briars as the angler walks along streams. Sometimes a net will catch, stretch out and deliver a fearsome blow to your back before you realize that the net is hung up. These net frames are made from laminated wood or aluminum. Wooden frames have aesthetic value and work well with bamboo rods. The inexpensive aluminum ones are less attractive; however, they will do the job. Both types of frames are fragile.

Smaller Accessories. A knife is an important item for fly fishing. Multi-purpose knives, such as Swiss Army knives, work best. A sharp blade is needed to clean your catch or perform minor surgery on a thorn embedded in your finger. A knife containing scissors, an awl, file and screwdriver can be a real asset.

Nail clippers are also essential. They are used primarily to clip tag ends after tying leader knots and flies. Some clippers come with other attachments, such as a hook hone, tiny knife blade and needle point to clear hook eyes. Although these attachments can come in handy, a standard set of nail clippers is satisfactory.

Hemostats are also important. This surgeon's tool, which anglers sometimes call a forceps, is perfect for removing hooks. They simplify things when releasing fish and they help prevent painful injuries from species with sharp teeth, such as northern pike. Hemostats also flatten barbs when you need to fish with barbless hooks.

Polarized sunglasses are a must for the fly fisherman. Polarized lenses allow you to see into the water. They also provide comfort when the sun glares on the water. When you're scanning the flats for bonefish or looking for trout in holding patterns, polarized sunglasses work great. Individuals who need prescription lenses should consider purchasing prescription polarized sunglasses for fishing. Inexpensive clip-ons, which flip up and down and fit over existing eyewear, are also available. You should tie them to the center of your eyewear frames with some monofilament—a sudden gust of wind can blow clip-ons off rather easily.

If your knife or clippers don't have one, you will need some type of hook hone or file in your kit. Sharp hooks are a must—even hooks that are perfect when you first cast need some "touching up" while astream. This is because flies, both underwater and dry, can hit stones or other hook-dulling impediments. Catching a number of fish on a fly can take the keenness from a hook point, too. A small hone works best because it's lighter in weight and can be used for both large and tiny flies.

One of the best ways to meet your leader needs is to carry a leader dispenser. This small, handy item holds five or six separate

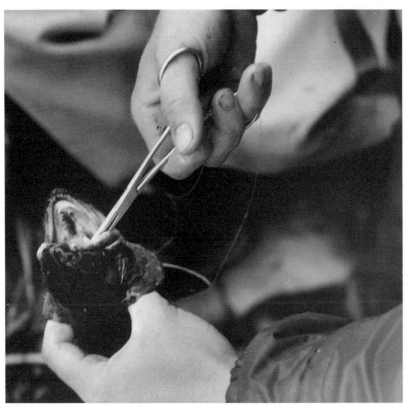

Using hemostats makes hook removal easy and safe. If used properly, hemostats also help prevent damage to the fish.

monofilament containers (flat ones are best) varying in size. Just add two or three full-length leaders and you're ready.

Unless you fish close to your vehicle or some type of shelter, you will need foul-weather gear. Waders protect the lower half of your body; however, it is easy to get soaked from a sudden summer shower. This can be miserable—even dangerous if fishing in high altitudes where hypothermia can result. A hooded poncho or light rain jacket can protect you from rain and provide comfort.

Finally, every angler should have some basic first-aid items. Band-Aids and disinfectant or antibiotic ointment are key items, as well as aspirin, toilet paper and a folding drinking cup. Waterproof matches, sun screen, insect repellent, iodine tablets (to treat water) and a small compass also are helpful to anglers in emergency situations. These items can be easily stored in a quart-

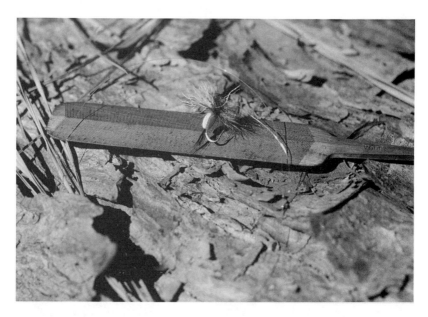

A file or hook hone is essential in keeping your hooks sharp. Hooks can hit rocks or other hook-dulling objects when fishing; sharpening hooks astream is sometimes a must.

sized, heavy-duty sealable plastic bag that is readily accessible.

The Vest. A vest is essential for most fly-fishing methods, especially wading. Lee Wulff popularized the vest early in his career with a hand-sewn one. In the ensuing half century, the vest has become standard wearing apparel for legions of fly fishermen. Many companies manufacture vests, and there are hundreds of designs available.

Strength—tough cloth and sound stitching—is a must. The average fisherman puts 10 to 15 pounds or more of gear into a vest. In order for the vest to be durable, there should be double thicknesses of material (usually cotton or a cotton/synthetic blend) at all stress points. These points include the shoulders, underarms, pocket and zipper areas. Particularly important is the way D-rings attach to the vest (at least two or three should be attached). D-rings should be securely sewn on the vest; tearing or ripping a D-ring off should be nearly impossible.

Numerous pockets are beneficial; however, pocket size and convenience are more important than quantity. Most vests have a sufficient number of pockets, but be sure to check their locations and sizes. Every pocket should close either with a zipper or with

Velcro. The vest pockets should also be expandable.

A vest should be capable of holding other accessories, such as clippers and hemostats. D-rings are used for this purpose. Most anglers attach a D-ring in the top center of the vest's back and one on a left-side breast pocket. Some vests have a roomy storage pocket across the back that will carry items such as your first-aid kit, rain jacket or small camera. Some modern vests now offer a built-in hooded poncho in the large back pocket.

Vests vary in length. If you fish deep, powerful waters where chest waders are used, the standard vest length may be a problem. Most standard vests come down to the waist and will most likely get wet. Chest-level "shorty" or "cut-off" vests are available and the properly designed ones carry a lot. Some of these also feature "zip-on" additions that make them into standard length vests.

The vest is an all-purpose storage unit—the fly fisherman's tackle box. There are some alternatives available, although not as versatile as the vest. One is the chestpack-backpack combo. It rotates around the body, enabling the angler to reach items in the backpack; it also puts the carrying weight on the shoulders—not the neck. This pack works great on long hikes into some back country or when you need to carry a lunch, some light walking boots and a change of socks. A second storage option is the chest

An alternative to the standard vest is the combination backpack and chest-pack. This contraption rotates around the body and puts the carrying weight on the shoulders.

fly box. This is used in hot weather when a vest would be uncomfortable (although mesh vests help alleviate this problem) or when the angler is fishing close to his transportation vehicle.

Non-Essential Accessories

If you are a gadget freak, there are enough fly-fishing accessories available to keep you extremely happy for a long time. They range from truly exotic to quite practical.

Fly, Line And Leader Treatments. These treatments include flotants, sinking solutions, absorbent granules for drying flies, line cleaners and leader straighteners.

Flotants, which are considered the most important, come in several forms. Spray containers are easy to use but they waste a lot of flotant. They are also quite heavy. Liquid solutions work well, but they too are wasteful. It's almost inevitable to spill a drop or two when dunking a fly in the solution, and significant spills happen easily when the bottle is left open. There also is a pollution factor. The solution causes a slick, oily film to form on the water.

Paste flotants are best. A touch of paste rubbed between your thumb and index finger and transferred to a fly is all that is required. A small container of flotant paste is light and will last a long time.

Drying granules work well, especially on slime-soaked flies; however, they are somewhat of a nuisance to use and very time-consuming—you could probably tie another fly on in a shorter amount of time. An easier method is to thoroughly rinse the fly in the lake or stream, vigorously shake it a few times and then blow the remaining moisture off. This approach should also work well with dry flies in the absence of flotants, especially if the flies have been prepared in advance. Advance preparation means treating dry flies with flotants at home before venturing on fishing trips. If you use paste flotants, an invisible protective coating forms on the hook and hackle which helps prevent corrosion.

Sinking solutions enhance saturating action and are used on wet flies, nymphs and streamers. Some solution rubbed on the leader also helps. Alternatively, you can use saliva to dampen your flies or hold them beneath the surface until fully saturated. If using split shot or a sinking line, this will not be a factor.

Lines used to be dressed regularly to protect them from rotting and keep them afloat. Today, most lines have a protective coating that provides lubrication for "shooting" through the rod guides with little friction. Most of these coatings, however, have a terrible antipathy for insect repellents. If a repellent comes in contact with a line, the coating literally melts away before your eyes. Dressings are useful when you're fishing waters with a lot of algae, pollen from blooming trees, flowers, slime or other materials that can accumulate on your line. Under these circumstances, an occasional cleaning will help the line perform at maximum efficiency.

Leader material, especially for tippets, kinks easily. Even stiff monofilament will kink if stored on a reel for a long time. You can straighten monofilament by pulling it between your fingers under pressure. There are also various commercial devices available for straightening purposes. Most devices feature some kind of soft leather or suede and are rather expensive. Here are two alternatives: a small piece of rubber from an old inner tube or a piece of leather from a worn out pigskin shoe or suede garment.

Tying And Threading Gimmicks. Numerous devices that tie basic fly-fishing knots are available. Most work reasonably well; however, learning to use them is about as difficult as mastering the particular knot they tie.

Various magnifying and illuminating devices that help anglers who are far-sighted or have difficulty tying on small flies under low-light conditions are quite beneficial and easy to use. These include fly threaders, which get the tippet through the eye of small flies; jeweler's loupes or other magnifying devices (many find a separate pair of glasses best), which help when close work on tiny flies is necessary; and small lights, which are used at dawn, dusk or night.

Aids For The Amateur Entomologist. Fly fishermen should learn what certain fish species eat, as well as other information that may assist in matching a hatch. Small aquarium-type nets for capturing insects from the surface, larger roll-up nymph nets or even devices that catch flying insects are available teaching tools. Devices that catch flying insects range from bulky contrivances to more convenient ones that attach to your rodtip. Flying insects, however, usually can be captured in your hand, hat or cap.

A more useful item is a stomach pump. This is a syringe-like device that sucks up water into the tube's bulb and squirts the water into the fish's stomach through its mouth. The water is then drawn back into the syringe. When the water is siphoned out of

Mayfly hatches are one of the most common insect hatches around water. Heavy hatches often set fish on a feeding binge.

the fish's gullet, insects or other food will also be drawn up. (Another approach is to dress the first fish you creel after it's landed. Slit the fish's stomach with a knife and examine the contents.)

Various color guides are also available to help in selecting the right pattern to match a hatch. Likewise, numerous ring-bound waterproof manuals exist to help identify a given hatch and provide information on duplicating patterns.

Other Items. One of the most important items not yet discussed is the creel. Basket or wicker-type creels have the appeal of tradition. They also can carry your lunch if you plan to hike into a remote area to fish. "Arctic" creels, which are soaked in water from time to time and use evaporation to keep the fish cool, are another alternative. For smaller fish species, a gallon-sized, sealable plastic bag will work if it's not too hot.

An assortment of other devices exists. Streamside tying kits can come in handy when nothing in your fly box matches a major hatch. Small pliers and scissors also have their advocates, but hemostats can substitute for the former and a Swiss Army knife carries a miniature version of the latter. Leader gauges will tell you diameter; however, this information is usually on the monofilament spools. Tape measures can be helpful if you like to know the exact length of released fish or if you need to measure one to be sure it is a "keeper."

A final item you should seriously consider is a camera. Cameras are now available in compact, relatively inexpensive forms, offering surprisingly high quality. A few snapshots of a treasured day astream can help preserve it for repeated and pleasant resurrection in the future. This is also the perfect way to ward off comments from skeptical friends about that "supposed" trophy you caught and released. With plastic fish mounts now available, you can take some quick measurements, snap two or three photos of a "fish of a lifetime" and eventually see an exact replica of the trophy on the den wall. If you carry a camera in your vest, be sure to protect it and your rolls of film in a sealable plastic bag.

Necessities, luxuries or somewhere in between, the paraphernalia of fly fishing is part of its appeal. Ultimately, each angler must decide for himself what he needs.

Putting It
All Together

7

The Elements Of
Casting

Mystery and mystique surround the art of fly casting. "Outsiders" are convinced that achieving a reasonable level of casting proficiency is a tedious, time-consuming process that creates more frustration than fun. To make matters worse, "insiders" who have already undergone their rites of passage into the sport contribute to the myth that effective fly casting is an art attainable only by the select few. Nothing could be further from the truth.

After a few hours of "hands on" instruction and practice, fly-fishing beginners can cast 30 to 40 feet consistently with decent equipment. This distance will catch the majority of fish discussed in this book. There are much higher levels of casting competence in fly fishing, which attracts skilled anglers. Adding distance, mastering certain intricacies of casts and understanding casts in specific situations are challenges for a lifetime.

When learning to cast a fly, timing is essential; timing—not strength—produces fish. Most anglers learning to cast force the action. In a smooth cast, the rod—not the caster—does most of the work; however, the caster controls the distance, line speed and motion timing through the rod.

Readying The Rod
Before casting, you need to mount the reel, put the rod sections together and string the rod. First, seat your reel with the reel handle on the side you prefer to reel. Then join the rod pieces

"Hands on" guidance is often advantageous when learning to cast. An open lawn also makes an excellent practice site.

The Elements Of Casting

Rod Assembly

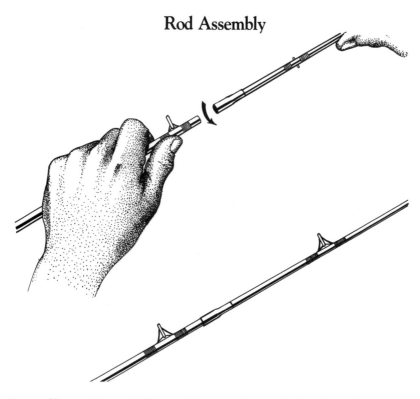

In assembling a rod, you should insert the butt into the tip with the guides 90 degrees misaligned, then twist the butt while aligning the guides until tight. This helps ensure the tip will stay attached. (To take the rod apart, untwist the rod while pulling.)

together starting at the butt section and progressing to the tip. It is best to insert each section's line guides at a 90-degree angle from the previous section's guides. After each section is in tight, align the guides. Dismounting or breaking down the rod should be done by reversing the process. This process can harm some fly-rod ferrules so make sure to read and follow the directions that accompany your rod.

Incidentally, here are a few words of warning on mounting and breaking down the rod: Do not lubricate metal ferrules, which are commonplace on older rods, by rubbing them alongside your nose; body oils can harm the metal over time. Do not force two sections together with undue pressure; forcing them can "blow out" the ferrules. Finally, if two sections of a rod are difficult to separate, seek assistance from a fishing buddy.

When stringing the rod, make sure the line leaves the reel at the proper place. Then pull out enough line so you are two feet past the leader and double the line back on itself. Push the doubled line through the guides. If the line slips, it will catch during this procedure. This is better than pushing the line through the guides with the leader, making a mistake and watching the line slide back out through all the guides.

Now you are ready to tie on a fly. To practice in the yard, break or file off the hook's "bend" portion, leaving only the hook shank. Tie on the fly. It's important to use a fly when practicing because its wind resistance makes a big difference in the mechanics of the cast.

Casting

There are four basic casts: the standard cast (also called the overhead, overhand or forehand cast), the backhand cast, the roll cast and the side cast. Other casts, such as the double haul, "S" (curve), "bow and arrow," steeple and splash (or splat), are for special situations and can be learned once you have mastered the four basic casts.

The four basic casts have similar elements. The weight of the fly line makes fly casting possible. The cast begins when the angler

The proper way to string up a rod is doubling the line as it is inserted through the guides. It will catch if you accidentally drop it during the process.

grasps the grip like he would in shaking someone's hand. The grip, which is usually made of cork, must be held firmly but not tightly. The angler's thumb should extend forward pointing toward the rodtip. There are two other grips that are sometimes used, but they are less common and inferior.

One is basically the same grip described above; however, the thumb is wrapped around the rod rather than extended toward the rodtip. The second grip uses the index finger instead of the thumb, extending it toward the rodtip. This weakens the casting motion and distance; however, it is acceptable for short, delicate casts. Generally, you should use the grip with the thumb extended or to the side.

Next, pull 20 feet or so of line from the reel with your free hand. (Once you've learned to cast, you will do this in rapid fire fashion while false casting until the desired amount of line is obtained.) An alternative, which is learned when accumulating line on retrieves or taking up slack in moving water, is to work line back out from your off-hand or to "shoot" it (explained later in the chapter) on the final power cast, sending the fly to its intended destination.

Once some line is out, begin moving the rod for casting motion. During this motion the line's weight offers resistance causing the rod to bend. This is called "loading the rod." The flex in the rod eventually resists the bend. As the bend straightens out, it sends (casts) the line through the air. In a standard forehand cast, this occurs once on the backcast and once on the forward cast. In this process, the rod acts as both a spring and lever.

The fly-fishing newcomer should develop the skills needed in executing the four basic casts. The most significant of these casts is the forehand cast. When you add the backhand cast, the roll cast and the sidearm cast to your repertoire, you should be prepared for some serious fishing. Collectively, these four casts enable anglers to meet most fishing situations encountered, although special conditions may require less common and often more difficult casting motions.

The Basic Casts

Overhead Cast. This is the fundamental cast and it involves the stroke or motion you will use on most other casts. Once you develop the rhythm and understand the cast, other approaches

This angler casts a nice loop while wading. Movement and timing are the most important casting skills a fly-fishing newcomer must learn.

should come fairly easily. With the overhead cast, beginners usually work too hard and too fast. The rod should do the work, resulting in a languid, fluid casting motion.

Movement and timing are the first elements that casters should master. For example, when to end the backcast and when to start the forward cast, as well as the arm movements involved in each, are extremely important skills in successful casting. Fortunately, these skills are not that difficult to learn. Try moving 20 feet of line that's suspended in air behind and in front of you in a smooth, steady motion. Your goal is to keep the line above your head at all times. (Both the forward and backward motions should be quite similar.)

When casting, compare the rod with the hour hand on a clock. You should move to 11 o'clock on the forward motion and to 1 o'clock on the backward movement. Do not go beyond 10 or 2 o'clock. If you're right-handed, remember to hold line in your left hand as you move the rod with your right. You should always have line in your free hand, except when playing a sizable fish on the reel.

Once the rod is "loaded," the continued, coordinated movement of the rod controls everything. You can move the rod from one end of the arc (just described) to the other with great purpose and power or slow, smooth motions. Both will work; however, as more line is let out, the movement speed becomes increasingly important. Again, timing is everything. This includes not only the timing of rod movement through the casting arc but also the pauses between loading the rod at the arc's front and back ends.

The timing of pauses determines the shape of the loop made as your line moves through the air; this loop's shape determines how well you perform as a caster. A good, tight loop on both the cast and backcast means less air resistance and less likelihood of the cast "falling apart." Visualize the loop as a tight "U" in shape; the legs of the "U" should change in length as the line moves through the air. By moving your head without moving your feet, you can see if the "U" is forming on both the cast and backcast. Watching the backcast can help solve many problems or "neaten" up your motion.

The rodtip is the focus of casting. When you stop and start the rodtip, you begin to create the loop. The line will do what the motion of the tip "tells" it. An excellent tool for casting practice is a short rod with a strand of bright-colored yarn attached. You can either purchase such a rod or make one by tying a piece of knitting thread to the tip of a two-piece rod. The motion created with this tiny outfit will show what you are doing right (and wrong) when casting. It will also enable you to analyze casting elements because the motion is readily visible.

Along with the arm motions involved in casting, foot positioning is also important. For most situations, your left foot (if you are right-handed) should be slightly in front of your right, and you should open your shoulders up toward the direction you want the cast to travel.

Theories on the "proper" way to cast are endless. You can find loads of information justifying a locked wrist (or a loose one), keeping your arm tight against your body and so on. Theories are

Casting Motion: Forward

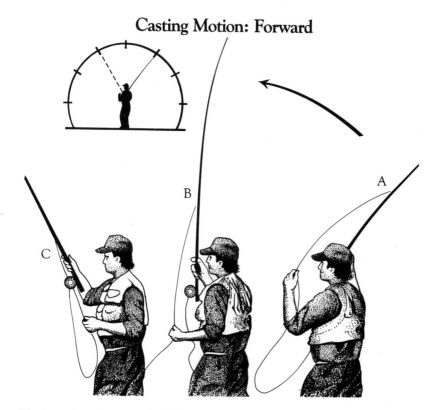

The forward casting motion should begin at 1 o'clock (A), move forward (B) and end at 11 o'clock (C). The direction of force is always forward.

all well and good, but it's what works for you that's important. In a way, casting is like a golf swing. You can analyze and criticize as much as you want, but the final judgment on any technique is simple: Does it work?

With your fly rod in hand, practice casting in the backyard or a nearby open field. If convenient, practice at a pond or stream. Alternatively, take a casting class. Fly shops, adult education programs, outfitters and other outlets offer these classes. A little research and a few calls should provide you with class information.

If you take a class, you should have classmates with comparable skills; make sure the class instruction includes plenty of "hands on" casting training; and ask if you will actually handle a rod on the water, and, if so, the amount of class time dedicated to this activity—the more the better.

Once you have learned the overhead cast, you are ready to learn the other three basic casts.

Backhand Cast. The backhand cast is merely an ordinary forehand cast performed across your body. It is nothing more than a cast where your arm extends across your body rather than to the side. Use of the wrist becomes more important on the backhand cast, because there is a more limited range of motion for the arm; you will not get as much distance with the backhand cast.

Still, casts of up to 50 feet are quite possible, and you will encounter situations where the backhand cast is vital. These situations are common when fly fishing smaller streams with brush or trees behind you; a forehand cast is usually out of the question.

An alternative to backhand casting is ambidextrous casting. For those fortunate few who are truly ambidextrous, this is the logical path to take.

Roll Cast. You will often find yourself in positions where a normal backcast is out of the question. Trees or a high bank are directly behind you, a strong wind may prevent the use of false casting, false casting may spook fish or you are too tired to false cast. In these situations, roll casting is advantageous. It is also best to cast heavily weighted flies, such as those that have lead split shot for eyes, with the roll cast. Once you've whacked yourself in the back of the head with these missiles a few times, you'll understand why!

Roll casting must be done with some line in the water; the surface tension caused by the line making contact with the water helps load the rod. Raise the rodtip slowly to a position that is nearly vertical. The pickup must be slow. If not, you will jerk the line from the water, losing the contact.

When the tip is poised, power it forward with considerable impetus—much more than you would for an ordinary cast. Stop the rodtip as you would in a normal cast—the tip should be pointing in the intended direction of line flow with the stop coming close to horizontal. The line will literally "roll" out in an unfolding "U" curve. If the roll collapses, you probably powered the rodtip too far forward.

The roll cast is fairly easy to master, although distance is limited due to the amount of line that can be lifted to the surface and turned over. A longer rod helps; it gives the same mechanical advantage as a long lever.

Casting Motion: Backward

The backcast begins at 9 o'clock (A), moves through 10 (B) and 11 o'clock, begins the drift at 12 o'clock (C) and ends at 1 o'clock (D). The direction of force is always backward.

Side Cast. There are two types of side casts: forehand and backhand. Both entail repositioning the rod, as well as the entire casting motion, by 90 degrees. In other words, the casting motion throws the line and rod through the air parallel to the water's surface rather than perpendicular to it. Side casting works best when you fish streams with limbs overhead, need to get a fly under a dock or some brush or are in situations where even the tightest loop would encounter some obstacle.

Other Casts

Double Haul. This cast achieves greater casting distance. It is important in situations such as fishing in strong winds, fishing saltwater flats or fishing big salmon or steelhead rivers. Becoming adept at the double haul is awkward at first because you must con-

Roll Casting

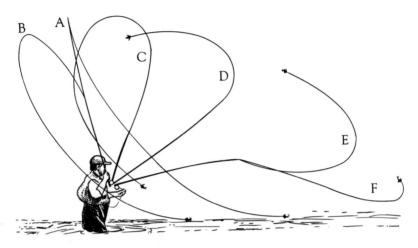

In roll casting, raise the rod vertically (A), allow the rod to drift past vertical and stop where the line hanging from the rodtip falls just behind your elbow (B), open your wrist and cast forward accelerating gradually (C), apply full power while gradually closing your wrist (D), stop hard and add a final flip (E) and roll the line out to its destination (F).

duct two motions at once: You must cast with one hand while jerking the line with the other to build up line speed. The faster the line speed, the greater the casting distance.

The double haul involves a quick line yank of 8 inches while picking up the fly to begin the backcast. When the backcast ends and you begin the forward cast, give a sharp pull (a bit longer than 8 inches) with your line-holding hand. In each case, you are tugging the line as the rod is being loaded; therefore, the line's speed is much faster. In learning the double haul, concentrate on the first motion, sometimes called a single haul, before adding the second step.

Bow-And-Arrow Cast. This special-purpose cast is used for exceptionally tight situations on small streams that are densely overgrown with vegetation. False casting and even roll casting are usually out of the question. When this is the case, hold the fly in your hand and use the flex in the rod to catapult the fly into close quarters. The distance achieved with this cast is only double that of the rod length.

Splash Or Splat Cast. This is a cast where the angler intentionally makes the fly land on the surface with considerable force—it

Complete Angler's Library

splashes or "splats" on impact. In bass fishing, this is a good cast to use when working shorelines where something is likely to "jump in" from the bank or fall from an overhanging limb. In trout fishing, the cast is primarily used with grasshoppers, which can land on the water with considerable force when a "hopper wind" pushes them into the water.

The splash or splat cast is easy to learn. You just finish a cast with more power than usual. As the leader turns over with the fly heading to the surface, pull the rodtip back a bit. After only a few minutes of practice, you should be producing satisfactory "crash landings."

"S" Or Curve Cast. Sometimes called a serpentine or snake cast, the "S" cast creates slack when the fly hits the water. In conflicting currents, this cast helps avoid drag. All you need to do is shake the rodtip from side to side as you complete the power stroke. This shivering motion causes the line to land on the surface in a series of S-shaped curves.

Other Special-Use Casts. There are many other casts you may want to learn as you gain experience. The steeple cast, forehand and backhand curve casts and a two-handed rod cast are among those that can prove useful.

Shooting Line

Adding distance to the final cast can be accomplished by "shooting" line. You will need to have extra line available in your hand (or possibly in a line basket or on a boat deck). Release it as the final forward cast, the power stroke, propels the fly toward its destination. As the power stroke is being completed, the angler releases the line at the point where he had been holding it in his free hand. The momentum of the line, which was in the air, "shoots" the additional line (held in reserve) out through the guides, adding distance to the cast. With sufficient line speed, especially if a weight-forward or shooting-head line is used, "shooting" can add appreciable distance to the cast.

Solving Common Casting Problems

Backcast Hitting The Water. When a backcast hits the water, your rhythm is interrupted and the drag robs your power. There are many reasons why line can hit the water behind you: taking the rodtip too far to the rear on the last false cast before making

"S" Casting

In executing the "S" cast, move the rod from side to side as you complete the cast. This creates slack when the fly hits the water. The "S" curves allow a drag-free drift.

the power stroke forward, dipping the rod too far back behind you when searching for power and delaying the beginning of the forward power stroke. Inadequate line speed on the backcast can also cause the line to hit the water. Finally, if using some type of weight-forward line, you cannot go much beyond the 30 feet of line where the weight is concentrated. If you do, the backcast will collapse.

The reverse of hitting the water on the backcast is hitting water during the forward motion of false casting. Not only does it cause the cast to break down, it spooks fish, too. The collapse of the forward cast usually happens when too much line is added to the cast prior to completion of the power stroke or the rodtip drops so low that the loop of the cast is destroyed. Do not drive the rodtip too low and avoid releasing too much extra line at once. You can, however, add a few feet of line to each false cast by feeding it into the cast at the proper time with the left hand.

Wind Knots. "Wind knots" are the bane of casters from beginners to the most experienced. Although adverse wind conditions can contribute to your "tying" overhand knots in the leader, they are usually caused by other factors. The most common of these is applying far more power to the finishing forward stroke (the one which will put the fly on the water) than necessary. If your fly is tangling on your line or leader butt with regularity, you are most likely applying too much power. Tipping the rod forward or allowing the tip to drift before you actually begin the forward power stroke can also cause wind knots. This happens if your timing is off when transferring from backcast to forward cast.

These "hard" knots are devastating to leader strength. An overhand knot effectively reduces the strength of monofilament by 50 percent. The knot is actually cutting into the leader.

Because most wind knots occur in the tippet, they can be fatal if undiscovered or left uncorrected when found.

It is often possible to "pick" the knot out. The point of your hook can be a useful tool in helping untie the knot. When the knot is already set beyond recovery, you should cut it out and retie the tippet leader.

Popping Flies Off. Popping off flies usually happens when the backcast drops too low and rocks are in the way. Flies also can be snapped off by beginning the forward cast before the backcast is completed. Similarly, weak backcasts that fail to straighten out the

False Casting: Forming the "U"

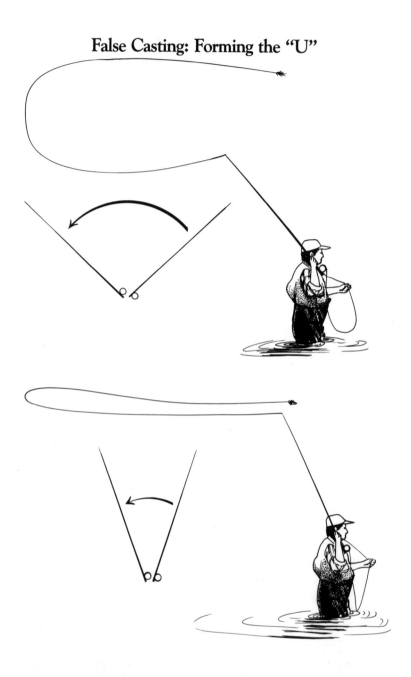

Loop control is an important aspect of casting. In false casting, a wide arc of power application causes a deep loop (top); a narrow arc results in a shallow loop (bottom). Anglers should practice casting frequently.

line can create this problem. You will not always lose the fly; however, there will be an audible "pop" similar to that made by a cracking whip.

Casts that strike the water too hard are caused from line that's too low when the cast is completed. This causes the line, leader and fly to collide with the water rather than turning over while still in the air. Pulling back on the rodtip as the cast is being completed can also cause "splash down." To avoid this, keep your cast a bit higher or make sure you stop the power stroke when the rodtip is still fairly high.

Casting mastery is an ongoing process. A willingness to try new approaches and test new casts is encouraged, and there is certainly much to be said for becoming a "backyard angler."

The motions and mechanics of casting can be fascinating, and some fishermen become so mesmerized by the process that they forget the real purpose of fly casting. It is not to look good, dazzle admiring onlookers or demonstrate how far you can propel a tiny bit of "feathers and fur." Casting is a means to a desired end— catching fish.

8

All About Knots

Tying knots is a skill that fly fishermen must learn and master. Knots are nothing more than connectors. Each knot "type" has a specific function; knots do not have all-purpose functions. It is vital that fly fishermen know what knots to use, when to use them and how to tie them. They can be divided into basic categories based on function. Some of the basic knot functions are attaching line or backing to reels, tying on flies, linking both backing and leader to line, joining sections of leader or tippet and leader together and attaching shock tippets or droppers.

Attaching Line Or Backing To Reels

The best knot used to attach your line or backing to the arbor on a reel's spool is the Duncan loop (sometimes called the uni-knot). It is a weak knot that ties the line on itself and slides under pressure. Sliding along the line is important; it allows you to snug the line down on the reel spool. Pass the end of the line or backing around the spool and bring the tag back out parallel to the line. In doing this, allow yourself 8 to 10 inches to complete the knot. Holding the tag end, bend it back toward the spool to form a loop between the two strands of line. Next, starting at the end closest to the spool, make five wraps with the tag end around both strands, passing the tag end through the loop as you complete each wrap. Finally, pull steadily on the tag end to draw the wraps together. When you want to replace a line or backing, you can

Duncan Loop

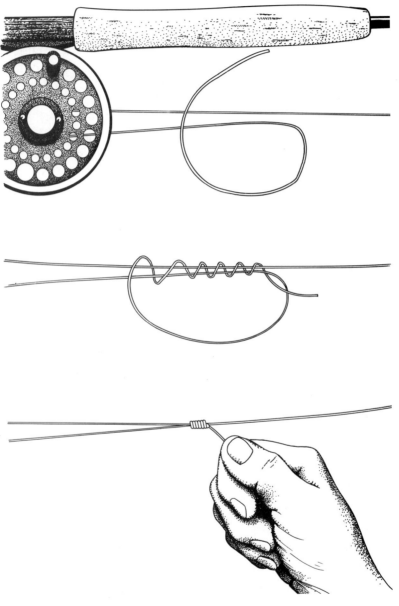

The Duncan loop, or uni-knot, is a popular knot; however, it lacks in strength. It is commonly used to attach the line or backing to the reel spool's arbor. Here, it is illustrated in three steps, showing its formation.

All About Knots   97

either cut the knot loose or work it back up from the reel arbor by reversing the sliding action.

Connecting Line And Leader

Linking two lines that are different in size and flexibility can be a problem. The following two knots connect a leader to line or backing to line. The simplest knot in this category is the tube knot (sometimes called a nailless nail knot). Substitute a hollow 2-inch tube, such as a section of a common soda straw, for the traditional nail. Lay the fly line against it with the tag end to the right. Place the butt section of your leader alongside the tube with its tag end to the left. Make sure you have 12 to 15 inches of leader (or backing) left to form the knot.

Hold the line and leader tightly against the tube with one hand while wrapping the leader's tag end around the tube, fly line and itself. (You are in effect reversing directions, working from left to right.) Keep each wrap tight against the previous one. (although they are separated for clarity's sake in the illustration). Use your fingers to keep the wraps tight.

After six wraps, push the leader's tag end back through the hollow tube. Now switch hands, without unraveling the wraps. Use your left hand to pull the tag end of the leader through the tube. Gradually remove the tube by sliding it to the open end (left). Pull gently on the leader's tag end, while maintaining pressure on the wraps, until the wraps begin seating on the fly line. As the wraps tighten, slide them down to the end of the fly line. Pull the tag end and main part of the leader simultaneously to complete the seating process. Trim the knot and coat it with rubber cement. The coating strengthens it and makes it flow easier through the rod guides.

One word of caution: This knot eventually causes the line behind the knotted leader to deteriorate. The entire line, however, is usually ready for replacement before this type of breakage occurs.

If you are having difficulties with this knot, there are acceptable, albeit inferior, alternatives that connect leader and line. A short, stiff piece of metal that has two or three barbs and an eye similar to a hook's on one end will work. Insert this needle-like device into the core of your line until only the eye protrudes. The barbs keep it from slipping back out, and the leader can be tied

Tube Knot

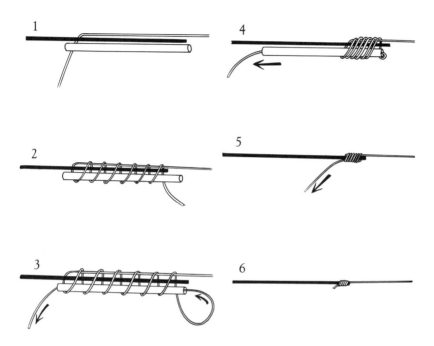

The tube, or nailless nail, knot is the simplest knot for linking two lines different in size and flexibility. It is commonly used to connect a leader to line or backing to line. Here, it is illustrated in six steps, showing its formation.

directly to the eye with an improved clinch knot. It is, however, extremely difficult to get the device centered in the fly line; in some lines, it is impossible to get it all the way down to the eye!

A connector called a "leader-link" is better. It is an elongated plastic bubble with holes at both ends and an opening in the middle. The leader and line are respectively inserted in the opening. An overhand knot (the simple "hard knot" most children learn to tie before tying their shoes) tied at the tag ends of both the line and leader can be snugged down inside the leader-link. This prevents the line and leader from pulling free. Leader-links work well if they are the right size for the line you're using.

Leader Knots

The blood knot and the surgeon's knot both connect leader

pieces together well; however, each knot has its own advantages and disadvantages.

The blood knot is the most widely used for uniting two strands of leader material, tying on a tippet and tying custom leaders. A blood knot is really two clinch knots (explained later) tied against one another: Lay two pieces of leader material across each other to form an "X." Leave 3 to 4 inches of overage. Wrap one monofilament piece around the other about three to four times; pull the tag back through the position where the leader pieces originally crossed and hold it there. Next, wrap the other leader piece around the opposite strand, making sure your wraps go in the opposite direction (think of them in terms of clockwise and counter-clockwise) of the first ones. Bring the tag back through the original opening where the two pieces crossed. Tighten the knot by pulling gently on each of the tags simultaneously.

Here are two other tips that make the blood knot easier to tie: Use your teeth to hold the tag ends; it frees your hands and prevents the tags from slipping. Put a bit of saliva on the knot; it makes the knot tighten easier and helps avoid scorching which weakens the leader.

Blood Knot

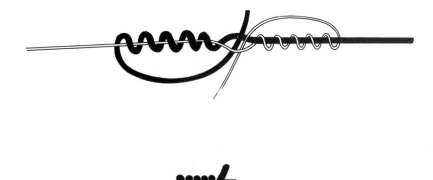

The blood knot is the most common knot used for connecting two leader strands, tying on tippets and tying custom leaders. Here, it is illustrated in two basic steps, showing its formation.

Complete Angler's Library

Surgeon's Knot

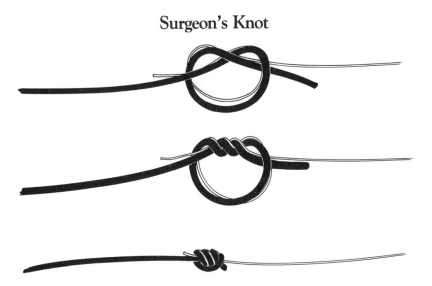

The surgeon's knot is easy to learn. It connects monofilament pieces with different diameters and links braided-wire monofilament (used in saltwater fishing). Here, it is illustrated in three steps, showing its formation.

The blood knot keeps the leader in a straight-line relationship. It can be tied with short strands of material and clipped off tight without weakening. Do not use a blood knot, however, to unite two strands of different diameters.

If you have two monofilament pieces with different diameters (for example, when attaching a shock tippet), you may want to tie an improved blood knot: Double the small piece of monofilament and wrap it around the larger strand five or six times. After wrapping, bring it back between the two strands. Then, wrap the large-diameter monofilament around the doubled line three or four times and bring it back through the loop (where the two leader pieces meet) in the opposite direction. Moisten the knot and pull it slowly to tighten.

The surgeon's knot, which is not actually used in surgical procedures, is one of the easiest knots to learn and tie. It can tie pieces of monofilament with varying diameters together and link braided-wire monofilament used in saltwater fishing.

The surgeon's knot is basically an overhand knot that uses both strands of leader at once. The strands are tied through the same loop twice. Sometimes, to prevent slippage and add strength, the material is passed through the loop three times. After passing the two monofilament pieces through the overhand knot's loop two or three times, pull all four pieces of monofilament simultaneously to tighten it. (Saliva helps in the tightening process.) Tying the surgeon's knot wastes more leader material, and it does not trim as close as the blood knot.

Knots For Attaching Flies

The knot selected for tying your fly to your leader is crucial. This knot is usually the culprit when things go wrong. This is also the knot you tie most often. The two knots described below are the ones the fly-fishing beginner should learn first.

Both the improved clinch knot and the turle knot are standard knots for tying on flies. To tie the turle knot, pull the fly onto the tippet, making sure the tag end enters the hook eye in the direction of the hook's point. Slide the hook a foot or so up the tippet and form a loop below it by tying a double overhand knot on the tippet. Bring this loop over the fly and secure it around (not on) the hook eye. When tightening the loop, do not catch any hackle in it, and the tippet's tag end must stay above the loop. When finished, the turle knot is actually tied on the fly itself.

The turle knot aligns perfectly with the actual fly. This can be advantageous when setting the hook, especially with tiny flies. Also, the fly always lands on the water the same way in relation to the line; whereas the improved clinch knot causes the hook to twist on the knot at different angles. The turle knot, however, needs quite a bit of tippet, and the excess tippet left around the hook eye after a fly is clipped off can be a nuisance. This "excess" can be extremely difficult to remove if you're using small flies and fine tippet material.

The improved clinch knot is used to tie on lures in several other types of fishing. In fact, the knot is so common that it is sometimes called the "fisherman's knot." To tie the improved clinch knot, insert 5 to 6 inches of the leader's tag end through the hook eye. Make five turns with the tag end against the leader, which remains behind the hook. Push the tag end through the loop formed just above the hook eye. If you stopped here and tightened the knot, you would have a simple clinch knot. To complete the improved clinch knot, you need to execute another step. After the tag end passes through the loop, a second loop will be

Turle Knot

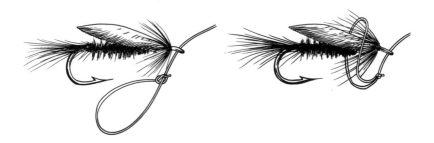

Improved Clinch Knot

The turle knot (top) and the improved clinch knot (bottom) are used for tying on flies. The turle knot aligns perfectly with the fly. The improved clinch knot (fisherman's knot) is popular in most types of fishing, including fly fishing.

formed. Pass the tag through this loop, lubricate the knot with saliva and tighten.

The improved clinch knot is difficult to tie with monofilament over 10 pounds. With heavier, stiffer leader material, four wraps, as opposed to five, should be sufficient to tighten the knot. Occasionally, especially when using 1- to 2-pound tippet material, the knot will slip or pull out. This knot also lacks the perfect alignment provided by the turle knot.

Loop Knots

In the past, loops often attached leaders to lines. Although this is not a popular method today, a basic knowledge of loop knots can be helpful. There are two easy-to-tie loop knots. For a permanent loop in the end of your fly line, which is most com-

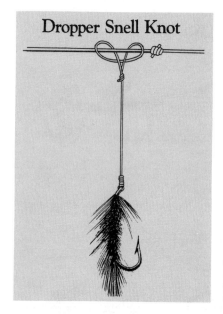

Dropper Snell Knot

The dropper snell knot does not require cutting and retying leader. It quickly fastens a snelled fly to a leader. This knot works well when fishing for small species like panfish.

monly used with monofilament fly lines or to attach backing, double the line back on itself to create the size loop desired. Then use two pieces of lightweight monofilament (5X or 6X) to tie separate nail knots, about a quarter inch apart, around the doubled line. This particular loop knot has no rough edges, so it slides through rod guides quite easily.

A simple loop knot can be created by doing nothing more than doubling the line back on itself and tying an overhand knot. This is really a simple (or half-finished) version of the surgeon's knot. It is not a very strong knot; however, it is easy to tie.

Alternative Dropper Knots

Once again, the best way to create a place for a dropper fly is to leave a lengthy tag on a blood knot (sometimes referred to as an extension blood knot). When using knotless leaders, however, or those that are pretied, it is easier to use alternative knots that do not require cutting and retying the leader.

One such knot is the dropper snell knot. If the fly is already snelled, simply tie a loop knot at the opposite end of the monofilament piece and snug the dropper above a knot in the main leader by bringing it back on itself through the loop. Alternatively, you can attach the dropper above a knot in the main leader by using an improved clinch knot (the same knot used to attach a hook) or a jam knot. For the latter, place the leader and dropper monofilament alongside one another. Wrap the dropper monofilament around the leader three or four times, then push its end back through the first loop. Pull the knot tight and trim.

The methods mentioned above are ineffective when using knotless leaders. This is because a knot is needed to keep the dropper from sliding. If working with knotless leaders, you should form a dropper attachment that would stay in place. This can be done by creating an improved dropper loop: Form a 3-inch loop in the leader and pinch the two crossing lines to make a loop. Then, twist it around the crossed lines five times. Open the center of the twisted lines and pass the loop through it. Use a finger or closed hemostats to keep the loop from pulling out, then tighten it. This loop enables you to attach the dropper.

A word of caution: An improved dropper loop weakens the main leader. Do not form one too close to the end of the leader, which is where monofilament is most susceptible to breakage.

Other Knots

There are specialized knots that the fly fisherman can probably learn as his skills advance. The Huffnagle knot, for example, is ideal for joining light monofilament to heavy material, such as when using a shock tippet. The Bimini knot, a double line with a loop used as a connector, is standard in saltwater fishing. The Trilene knot, a variation of the clinch knot, is useful for attaching large flies and bass bugs. The figure-eight knot works great for attaching braided wire material to a fly.

9

Knowing And Reading
The Water

Reading the water can be one of the most difficult skills to learn in fly fishing. The reason is simple: All the written materials and expert advice in the world cannot substitute for experience. First-hand observation and wisdom accumulated through years of fishing teach anglers how to read the water. Reading the water is, basically, knowing or sensing the location of fish.

There are some tips that provide guidance in learning how to read the water. Keep in mind, however, learning this skill greatly depends upon you putting in the time.

Other anglers can help you develop some of the requisite "reading" skills. Having a mentor accompany you on the water, point out likely holding spots, make occasional observations, such as "I've caught a lot of fish near that log over the years," and share outdoors knowledge can be invaluable.

Another excellent "teacher" is a scrupulously maintained diary. Write down facts and observations made about where fish hold and hit on a regular basis. Over time, your reasoning processes will begin to convey clear messages, such as "Fish here, it is a likely holding spot for brown trout."

Strategies and hints for locating specific fly-fishing species will be discussed in later chapters; however, some elements are universal for all fish. Fish are creatures of habit, and the most consistent and constant habit is the need for food. A keen knowledge of the dietary habits of fish results in successful fishing.

Carefully studying the water before making casts is important. It is beneficial to learn to read the water from an experienced angler; developing a mentor relationship can bring much success.

Knowing And Reading The Water

The Importance Of Food

Recognizing the types of places where fish would find food is the first step in reading water. The following questions should be asked: What are the principal items of diet? Are there certain times of the day or particular conditions when fish are more inclined to feed? Does most of their food come from the surface or beneath it?

Most fish that are readily taken on flies eat beneath the surface. Admittedly, there are few angling moments that can match the excitement of a smashing surface strike or a sipping rise from a monstrous fish; however, if a certain fish species gets 80 percent of its food below the surface, subsurface flies should be used.

It is also important to use flies that "fit" the fishing season. Matching the hatch works best. It makes no sense to cast terrestrial patterns, such as grasshopper or cricket imitators, in the early spring. A streamer that looks like a crayfish won't work in water containing no crayfish! Exercising common sense is extremely important when identifying available foods and terrestrials.

The Spawning Factor

Another universal fish habit is the instinct to reproduce. With a few specialized exceptions, such as hatchery-reared hybrids, all fish respond at the right time to nature's spawning ritual. These procreative habits consist of more than the actual acts of laying and fertilizing eggs. The pre- and post-spawn periods involve tense feeding for many species. Several species, such as bream, bass and crappies, are most easily caught during the spawning process. In fact, the spawning migration is the only time some fish, such as migratory salmon, can be taken on a fly rod.

Recognizing Habitat

Virtually all freshwater fish, as well as most saltwater species, spend the majority of their lives in or near cover. Cover offers three things: a hideout, a place of ambush and a resting spot.

Hideouts protect fish from enemies. These enemies can include other fish, snakes, various mammals (including man) and raptors. One of the most common stream hideouts is undercut banks where the current constantly erodes the shoreline, creating a watery cave. If there is a heavy stream flow, these "caves" will be abundant. The best caves are occupied by the biggest fish, and so

Eddies or backwaters are prime holding spots for fish, especially for species like brown trout. Fish prefer areas that allow them to be energy efficient.

on down the line to the small fry. A spot where you hook or land a big fish is most likely home to similar-sized fish throughout the season. Good "holes" are no accident; they have some unique feature that fish prefer.

Another common hideout is vegetation, such as weedbeds, massed lily pads, mangrove roots and moss. Rocks, logjams, jetties, riprap, shipwrecks, sunken brush piles, piers and docks also provide fish hideouts. Any time you see "structure," the generic term used to describe hiding places, investigate thoroughly.

Cover can also be used for ambushing. Many sportfish that eat other fish spend their time lying in wait for dinner. Again, structure is the key. It attracts predators in search of a meal, as well as baitfish in search of protection.

Fish frequently choose a particular stretch of water for reasons of energy efficiency. For example, anglers who fish for brown trout realize that they, especially seasoned old lunkers, love eddies or holding spots where the stream flow's force is diminished. Similarly, salmon will, in the course of their spawning migration, choose certain pools year after year. (This is even true of Pacific salmon that die at the end of the spawning process.)

Knowing And Reading The Water

Many fish-holding places fit all three habitat categories. These holding spots offer protection, food and a place to rest.

Knowing Where To Cast

Even if you recognize holding spots, you still must cast your fly in a realistic way. This means reading the water from a different perspective. You need to know the type of cast that will serve you best. With dry flies, it is important to avoid drag. You need to have the fly, whether surface or subsurface, in a location where food is commonly presented to fish. The retrieve speed should match the speed of the real-life organism you're imitating. For example, a streamer imitating a minnow might need to be stripped quite rapidly; one resembling a leech or lizard might be moved rather slowly.

In moving water, currents and counter-currents, merging runs, places where the stream runs against some obstacle and is driven back and numerous other special situations confront the angler.

All other things being equal, cast to the place most likely holding fish. In difficult situations, use simple casts before ones that increase the likelihood of hanging up, dragging or going awry in some way.

Water that appears to do one thing on the surface but behaves quite differently below the surface is the most difficult to read. Big, powerful rivers and some tidal waters are examples of this type of moving water. Careful observation can be beneficial. Watch how air bubbles behave. Look for quiet pockets amidst boiling or surging water. Note what is happening with any flotsam, live insects or baitfish you see. Most of all, pay close attention if feeding fish are visible.

Seeing fish feed is an integral part of reading the water. For example, frequent surface breaks in calmer water do not always mean fish are working on top. The breaks may come from the tails of fish, not their heads, as they feed on nymphs or emergers. If you repeatedly see dorsal fins instead of heads, fish are probably eating something just below the surface. Mud trails can reveal bonefish and drum. When you see fish, determine exactly how they are feeding; adjust your fly offering accordingly.

Reading still water is easier than reading moving water. Your main concern is finding the location of fish. Evaluating or reading the water makes quite a difference in your success ratio. Which

Seeing feeding fish is an important part of reading the water. Look for dorsal fins as an indicator of fish taking nymphs.

side of a stump is a big bass likely to prefer? Should the outer edge of a weed strip be worked before the inner side? What depth is ideal for the fly? The answers to these and other questions come, once again, from experience.

When fishing uncharted waters, do not be afraid to ask questions. Local knowledge can be an invaluable ally. Remember that the excellent angler is usually the one who experiments. Don't hesitate to change flies and tactics often until you find something that works. Finally, be sure you have a good pair of polarized sunglasses. These sunglasses enable you to see fish that would otherwise be invisible. You can see the "flashing" turns that often denote a strike, even though you feel nothing. The glasses also allow you to see structure better.

Knowing and understanding the water is a subtle skill. You should strive to learn something new every time you fish. One of the glories of fly fishing is that no matter how much time you devote to the sport, there will always be new waters to read and new things to learn in old, familiar waters.

=10=

Maneuvering In Or On The Water

Methods used to get within casting range of fish are often overlooked in fly fishing. Reaching this critical position may involve wading, walking a bank, paddling, rowing or poling a boat, using a trolling motor or gliding along slowly in a self-propelled float tube. All these approaches require stealth and savvy while maneuvering into position.

Watching an old hand and a rank novice wade a tumbling, slick-bottomed mountain trout stream side by side will reveal some major differences. The veteran most likely moves easily with little effort from one likely casting position to another while the beginner stumbles and staggers along toward less-than-optimum spots for casting. Experience plays a key role in these differences; however, other factors, such as equipment, can also be involved. A lot of fly fishermen fail to approach wading with the same attention that they devote to other aspects of fly fishing.

There are three basic types of wading: wading in hip waders, wading in chest waders and wading wet. Conditions will determine the proper approach. Wading wet can be pure pleasure on a hot summer day when water temperatures are in the 60-degree range or higher and air temperatures soar above 80 degrees. This situation can prevail almost anywhere, including the working of a mountain trout stream to a judicious probing of the flats for bonefish. It is unwise for anglers to wade wet in trout or salmon water

In warm weather, wading wet is a pleasant way to fish small streams. Wet wading is usually done when water temperatures are 60 degrees or more and air temperatures are 80 degrees or higher.

Maneuvering In Or On The Water

Hip boots are quite suitable for wading in small streams. If you plan to go deeper than your knees, however, you should wear chest waders.

up to the waist or beyond. If the water is cool enough to support these species, it will be uncomfortably cool once you are wet to the upper thighs or higher. In small streams, where you won't go deeper than your knees, hip boots are a suitable choice. Otherwise, you will want chest waders. Although not considered "wading," float tubing involves wet wading or the use of chest waders.

Tips For Safe And Successful Wading

In rough water, do not attempt to wade and cast simultaneously. Inch your way to a potential spot, firmly plant both your feet in the direction of your intended target and begin working out line. Sometimes, a midstream boulder or flow-breaker object will diminish water pressure, giving you more stability. These objects can also help hide your profile, decreasing your chances of spooking fish.

When wading in moving water, read the water for potential wading spots the same way you'd read the water for bream beds or salmon lies. You can also reach an area of the stream that few others fish by switching sides of the stream some distance from the hole. You can always retrace your footsteps to get back to the side of the stream from which you started. Using a little ingenuity in order to reach places where others seldom fish often pays handsome dividends.

Along heavily fished streams, for example, use approaches that the average angler would not try. This may mean easing along under limbs, stalking where others race madly ahead, switching from the roadside of an easily accessible stream to its opposite bank or resorting to an unorthodox casting position or motion.

Your wading technique is extremely important. More fish are spooked by inept wading than by sloppy casts. When fishing long, still pools, move through the water with great care. The same is true in glassy-smooth saltwater flats, lakes or ponds. Nothing spooks feeding fish more than a big wake or splash—unless it's banging and bumping rocks underwater. Fish cannot see you, at least when wading, beyond a distance of 40 to 50 feet; however, they notice a big ripple or an in-water disturbance at a much greater distance.

Wading deep can be advantageous. It lowers your profile and puts you more at "eye level" with the fish. It also improves your surface observation, even though it is more difficult to cast. A second approach is to ease out from shore gently and slowly, moving through the shallows with great care.

Use overhanging trees or brush at the edge of streams to camouflage your approach to a pool. Similarly, there is absolutely nothing wrong in stooping to conquer. Kneeling lowers your profile when casting to particularly finicky fish, and natural in-stream objects can act as camouflage or hideouts. If the fishing pressure on a given body of water is high, practicing stealth tactics will increase your success ratio.

Fish usually face upstream or into the current. This information is vital when positioning yourself to cast after wading. It is important in fast-moving streams, as well as tidal water or lakes with feeder streams entering still water. The best wading approach, however, is not always the one that has the angler moving upstream. In spring creeks, for example, fish may be exceptionally leader shy; a downstream cast that puts the fly in the fish's window of vision may be the best approach.

As a general rule, a wader should stay in the shade if possible. He should never let his shadow fall on the water area he will be

Sometimes wading waist-deep or even deeper is necessary. Ideally positioning yourself for a cast can mean the difference between success and failure.

casting to—even the shadow of a line during a false cast or from a rod can put fish down.

Skillful wading is a great equalizer. A fisherman who is an expert wader can make up for inadequacies in other areas, such as casting ability.

Always keep two basic truisms in mind when wading. First, cover the water close to you before attempting longer, more difficult casts. Whether casting to the edge of a bream bed, working shorelines for bass or working a long pool full of rising trout, the close fish take precedence. Avoid fish that race upstream in a panic; they spread that alarm to other fish.

Second, cover the entire water area from one point before wading to the next. Many anglers, for example, make a few casts, catch a glimpse of a rising trout at a distance and hasten off to greener angling pastures. Feeding fish are not taking the next waterway express to another county! Cover all the water, not just some of it.

Good wading skills will make you a better fisherman. Unlike casting, wading is not a skill where physical attributes loom large; you don't need to be a first-rate athlete or possess an exceptional sense of balance. An expert wader uses his head, studying each situation and analyzing every wading movement.

Good wading equipment, along with mental acuity, will help you achieve reasonable mastery of in-water maneuvers. No matter what type of wading equipment you use, you will need a good repair kit because sooner or later a sharp rock, limb or other object will puncture your wading props.

Hip Waders

Hip waders are used primarily in small streams. They are more comfortable than chest waders in warm weather; however, they have snaps that link to the wearer's belt, causing them to tug on your pants. There are two solutions to this problem: Wear a pair of heavy-duty suspenders to counteract the pull of the waders and transfer some of the weight to your shoulders or buy hip waders with a harness-like arrangement that suspends them from your shoulders.

Another problem with hip waders is that most of them, especially cheaper ones, have rubber-lug soles. Far from providing traction, rubber soles are an open invitation to get wet. Furthermore, glue does not work on these soles. Anglers, therefore, cannot attach felt or other non-skid material to help prevent slipping.

One solution to the "slipping" problem is to purchase boots with soles that accept glue. Do-it-yourself felt kits are readily available in most fly-fishing shops, or you can choose a cheaper but perfectly acceptable alternative: Cut two pieces of heavy-duty carpet to the shape of the soles and attach them to the soles with waterproof super glue (use clamps to hold the carpet in place until the glue dries completely). Most top-quality waders, which are more expensive, already have felt soles or metal studs.

Chest Waders

Chest waders are essential when fishing big rivers, still-water wading and float tubing. There are two basic types of chest waders: stocking-foot waders and built-in boot waders. Stocking-foot waders are preferable most of the time. They are more comfortable, less prone to leak, easier to repair when they do leak, more stable (because you are wearing separate, usually better, boots), available in various fabrics, easier to store (a pair of nylon stocking-foot waders can fold up neatly into a poncho-sized pouch) and, even when you add boots, lighter and less cumbersome than waders with built-in boots.

Stocking-foot waders are more expensive because you need to purchase wading boots, too. However, they are definitely worth it. "Getting dressed" is a little more time-consuming and tedious with stocking-foot waders. It involves layers in this order: a pair of socks next to the skin, stocking-foot waders, another pair of socks, gravel guards and wading boots. This extra time and effort, however, pays off in comfort and convenience in the water.

Stocking-foot fabric choices will depend upon the type of fishing, as well as when and where this fishing takes place. Nylon waders with neoprene feet that keep the toes warm are the best choice for spring, summer and early fall. (They can also be comfortable in winter if you wear insulated underwear, wool pants and warm socks under them.) For extensive cold-weather use or in big Western waters when the snow is still melting, insulated neoprene waders that are at least four millimeters thick work best. (These also are great for waterfowl hunting in duck blinds.) Insulated waders are not meant for hot-weather use; wearing them in hot conditions would be like wearing a bodysuit in a sauna!

Wading Boots
Wading boots or shoes should provide three things: traction, comfort and support. Felt or cleats (or the two mixed) usually supply the traction. Wading chains are also available for situations requiring cleats. These are useful in rivers with a lot of big, slick rocks; they are almost mandatory in streams with powerful currents. Wading chains, or clip-on cleats, are special devices that strap around your boots or "slip on" over them like galoshes.

Comfort will depend upon a good fit and weight. Boots that seem light when dry may weigh several pounds when wet. Support is particularly important in the arch and ankle areas. Other factors to consider are steel-reinforced heels and toes and the fastening method. There is a lot to be said for boots with two or three large Velcro straps instead of laces.

Both felt and cleat bottoms wear out long before a good pair of boots. Replacement kits are available, or you can make your own replacement soles. For casual wet wading in still water or small streams, wading shoes made from some old sneakers and carpeting work fine.

Author Jim Casada uses a homemade wading staff in a swift stream. Wading staffs provide support while you're maneuvering from one casting position to another.

Special problems exist in saltwater wading, such as razor-sharp coral or sand. Several wading shoes and sandals have been developed with the flats fisherman specifically in mind.

Other Wading Equipment

A wading staff provides extra support against the stream bottom as you wade from one casting position to another in rough waters. It can be clipped to your vest for convenience. A variety of commercial wading staffs, including collapsible ones and those with chain retractors, are available; however, homemade ones are easy to make and do the job. An old rake handle with a metal collar attached to the bottom for strength and a grip made from a leather thong or heavy cord is one example. Strong aluminum tubing, a ski pole or a good, stout stick all work, too.

Gravel guards are quite useful with stocking-foot waders. These handy devices snug tightly around the top of your boots, preventing sand and gravel from entering your boots. The best gravel guards are 6 to 8 inches wide, have metal hooks and zip close around your leg.

When wading in big streams or the ocean or when float tubing, you should wear an emergency flotation device. Losing your balance in a powerful stream can be dangerous; once you fall, regaining your footing can be extremely difficult.

Some vests are equipped with special CO_2 cartridges that can be activated in emergency situations; similar devices that can be worn around your wrist are available. Some chest waders have a built-in inflatable band around the top for emergency use. If you are wearing chest waders that do not fit snugly, make sure to wear a belt around the top of them. This prevents water from entering the waders if you take a spill. Finally, when wading potentially dangerous waters, you should be sure to have a fishing partner who's nearby.

The Floating Fly Fisherman

Though the popular image of fly fishing is an angler standing knee-deep in a pristine stream, many different watercraft are used for the sport. Two basic watercraft designs—poled flats boats and Mackenzie boats—are geared specifically for fly fishing. Canoes and johnboats are also used for fly fishing—even larger bass boats work for certain fish species and situations. Float tubes, which must rank along with graphite rods as a modern miracle for fly fishermen, are also very popular.

Float Tubes

Float tubes, or belly boats as they are sometimes called, enable anglers to wade farther out and work tight places. They are great in ponds, small lakes, back bays of large lakes and slow moving streams. Float tubes, however, have some limitations:

• They should not be used in moving water.

• They should not be used for fishing far out in large bodies of still water.

• They should not be used during warm weather in places where cottonmouth moccasins or alligators exist.

Light and easily transported when deflated, float tubes are use-

Float tubes are an asset when fishing in high-country Western lakes. When using float tubes, anglers must wear flippers for propulsion.

ful when backpacking into high-altitude lakes. They also come in handy in tree-choked sloughs. Float tubes are also less expensive compared to boats and great for stalking fish and giving anglers a new perspective.

A float tube should have a comfortable back rest that provides added flotation if a leak develops. Velcro flaps clamp your rod down, enabling you to work on other things, such as tying a knot or replacing a tippet. Zippered pockets are great for storing equipment. The "seat" area in the middle of the tube should be sturdy and comfortable, and the entire tube should have a strong, protective outer layer.

In addition to the float tube, you will need a pair of flippers, similar to those used by scuba divers, for propulsion. To move around in a belly boat, you need to do an upright imitation of a

Mackenzie boats are commonly used to get to remote pools on big Western rivers such as Montana's Bighorn. They are wide-hulled and extremely stable.

crayfish—paddle backward. Make sure to attach your flippers to your shoes or boots with some string; flippers do not float and can slip off your feet in heavy weeds. If you lose a flipper, you will need to "backstroke" with your arms.

Learning to use a float tube is easy. The only difficulty is getting in and out of the water. In each case, you usually move toward your destination backward. If you begin to stumble, you just sit down.

Canoes And Johnboats

Canoes and johnboats are ideal for fishing in moving water where larger craft cannot go. They are also easy to beach if you want to wade in a likely pool or shoal. Johnboats, however, should not be used in white water, and canoes should be used only by experienced anglers who can swim.

Noise can be a problem with these boats, especially if aluminum craft are used. Anglers should handle paddles carefully as well as having the bottom of their watercraft carpeted. Painting a craft's exterior reduces the metal's brightness.

Casting from johnboats and canoes is usually done in a sitting position. The cast's motions, however, are quite similar to the stand-up cast's motions; the necessary minor adjustments are easily made. Anchors can be advantageous, especially if you want to hold tight at the edge of a river pool, position your cast perfectly to a bream bed or fish a school of crappies. Small gasoline motors or electric trolling motors can be installed on both canoes and johnboats.

Special-Use Craft

Some boats are specifically designed for fly fishing. Flats boats, for example, have shallow drafts and sighting and poling platforms. They are popular with flats fishermen in the Florida Keys and elsewhere. Mackenzie boats, which are wide-hulled and supremely stable, have become popular on many renowned Western trout rivers such as the Madison, Bighorn, Snake and Yellowstone. The fly caster securely stations himself in the front of the boat using a specially cut groove that allows him to "lock" his thighs in place for balance. He then works the water from the front of the boat while his partner handles the oars.

Other Boats

Bass boats, as well as most larger saltwater boats, have things that can get in your way and create messy tangles. Specially made stripping baskets can offset this problem to a degree. Most boats will take you to fish that are otherwise unreachable—this is the most important function of a boat.

Pursuing
The Quarry

=11=

Starting With Panfish

anfish are the perfect target when learning how to fly fish. They are prolific, one or more species will most likely exist in the nearest body of fishable water and, best of all, they are exceptionally cooperative. Panfish hit a wide variety of fly patterns because insects are a major portion of their diet. Panfish are constantly hungry, so it should be fairly easy to find fly-fishing techniques that provoke strikes under almost all conditions.

Furthermore, panfish are quite forgiving when it comes to sloppy or less-than-delicate casts, and they are real battlers for their size. Because panfish tend to overpopulate, you are helping the species and lake when you keep them for the frying pan; they make delicious table fare.

Panfish Equipment

Virtually any balanced outfit will work for panfish, although some options are certainly preferable. A 4-, 5- or 6-weight rod is ideal, although lighter rods produce more of a fight with these feisty scrappers. Heavier rods, such as 7-, 8- or even 9-weight rods, work well if bass are in the area—sooner or later you will hook a big fellow. These rods are also beneficial in windy conditions or when a bit of extra casting distance is required.

The reel is nothing more than a line storage device when panfishing; drag and backing are irrelevant. Pertaining to lines, a floating line will suffice; however, sink-tip lines work well when

The author's daughter, Natasha, caught this chunky bream with a fly rod. Panfishing is a great way for newcomers to learn fly-fishing basics.

the fish are several feet below the surface. Double-tapered lines are a good choice. They are easier to cast than level lines, which are another suitable choice. You can also reverse a double-tapered line on the reel when it begins to wear out. Seven to 9 feet is ample length for your leader, and 4- or 6-pound-test line is fine.

Panfish Flies And Poppers

Panfish are, for the most part, eclectic feeders: They will eat just about anything. Crappies, which dine primarily on minnows, are an exception. In warm weather, surface patterns work well. Almost anything that floats tied on No. 8 to 14 hooks will draw strikes. Some excellent topwater choices include Sneaky Pete poppers (chartreuse and white seem to be the best colors), tiny deer-hair bugs and dry-fly attractor patterns, such as the various Wulffs (Royal, White and Blond). Terrestrial patterns also produce for panfishing. Some of these flies include sponge spiders, Joe's Hopper (a grasshopper imitation normally used for trout), Letort Cricket and red and black ants. Surface offerings work best when water temperatures increase during spring, during active hatches and at dawn and dusk throughout the summer.

Nymphs are the best choice for below-the-surface action; tiny streamer patterns can also be useful, especially for larger panfish that eat minnows. It is possible to fish tiny jigs ($1/16$- or $1/8$-ounce heads) with fly rods, although you usually just drop the jig into the depths and impart action instead of casting. Among the more versatile underwater panfish patterns are the Tellico Nymph, Hare's Ear, Pheasant Tail, small Muddler Minnows, San Juan Worm and scud (freshwater shrimp) imitators.

Panfishing Tricks And Approaches

Long-distance casting is not particularly important in panfishing. Casts ranging from 25 to 30 feet will suffice; you will seldom need casts of more than 40 to 45 feet. You will need, however, to "outwait" your quarry to get strikes. Panfish usually prefer stationary surface popping bugs or flies. When fishing lakes and ponds, do nothing to your offering until all the circles or ripples caused from its landing disappear. Then wait until you can no longer stand the inaction. A fish will often be lurking directly beneath the fly, and any movement will spook it!

"Working" the fly should be nothing more than a slight

This nice bluegill fell for a Sneaky Pete popper. Poppers work well as surface-action attractors for panfish.

twitch. This should be done with your free hand by pulling on the line. (If you work a fly with the rodtip, you usually put yourself in a difficult position to properly set the hook) After two or three twitches, retrieve the fly and cast again. You should have at least 30-second intervals between each cast; 60-second intervals are even better.

Panfish, except crappies, spend most of their lives near shore or in shallow water. This area offers cover that provides protection and food. Crappies tend to move around more, particularly in regard to depth.

Because panfish inhabit shallow, in-shore waters, they are easily caught by bank fishermen. Walking a farm pond's banks, especially in a pasture or grassy area with little shoreline vegetation, can be a pure delight. You cover 2 to 3 feet of water each time you take a step and cast. If a backcast is impossible, use a roll cast.

Another approach is wading for panfish. This is common in smaller streams. Wading wet in summer's heat can be both refreshing and productive. Usually, stream panfish concentrate in deep eddies, still pools or shady spots beneath undercut banks. You can also wade in shallow ponds or lakes; however, be prepared for sudden drop-offs if water clarity is poor.

The most versatile approach is fishing from a boat, canoe or float tube. A canoe or small johnboat powered by paddles or a small trolling motor is ideal. You just ease along parallel to shore while casting to potential spots. Front and back anchors help maintain a stationary position in productive spots or when casting to bedding fish.

In still water, a float tube is the best vessel for fly fishermen. It enables you to move within easy casting distance with minimal disturbance. You can also move into shallow, tight places that even a canoe could not enter.

Double Trouble For Panfish

Although tandem rigs require greater casting skill and occasionally produce leader tangles, they can double your panfishing pleasure. The approach simply allows you to fish two flies at once. Several combinations, such as two floating flies, a floating fly with a dropper nymph or two underwater flies, work. When using a floating fly (or bug) and a nymph, the surface fly acts as a bobber or strike indicator. If it suddenly moves or jerks under the surface, set the hook.

There are two methods to rig tandem flies. One is to tie about 2 feet of tippet to your leader, leaving 6 to 8 inches of the larger monofilament piece as a tag end after tightening your blood knot. One fly is tied to this tag; the other to the end of the tippet. When a dry fly (or bug) and nymph combination is used, tie the surface fly to the heavier piece of leader material. There should be at least a 4-pound test difference between the two monofilament pieces. This difference helps ensure that the heavier, stiff material will remain separate from the main leader, decreasing the chances of tangling.

The second rigging method removes the need for different-sized leader material and makes casting easier. Tie the fly or popper to the leader's end. Connect a piece of leader material that is

Tandem rigs spell "double trouble" for bluegills. They also work well when fishing for trout and other species.

the same weight or lighter (not more than a 2-pound difference) and 15 to 18 inches long to the hook's bend with an improved clinch knot. Then attach the dropper fly.

Cast both tandem rigs the way you would cast a single fly. These rigs require some extra effort, especially if using big-bodied poppers. The increased wind resistance makes casting seem awkward, and the flies hit the water with more force. When fishing two flies, notice and remember which one draws most or all the action. If your strikes are happening because of a particular fly pattern, use the same pattern for both flies on your rig. If all the hits are on the surface or underwater, remember the pattern!

Tandem rigs are also used for "mixed-bag" fishing. The lead fly, for example, can be a big bug or popper for bass while the dropper is a small one for panfish.

Tandem Rigs

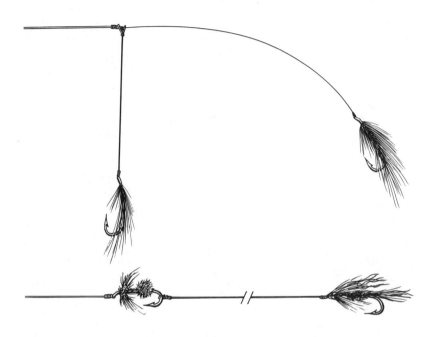

Both of these tandem rigs should be cast in a way that's similar to a single-fly rig. Even though they require some extra effort, the blood-knot tandem rig (top) and the straight-line tandem rig (bottom) help anglers catch more schooling fish.

Bluegill Methods

Bluegills, the most popular panfish species, thrive in farm ponds, small lakes, large reservoirs and moving water. Water purity, clarity and temperature do not play important roles in the bluegill's habitat selection.

The best time to fish for bluegills is during their annual spawning period. This period varies across the country; however, the traditional spawning peak is during May. The peak is earlier in the deep South and later in northern climates. Bluegills congregate in large numbers to spawn. Males fan out saucer-shaped depressions, or beds, for females to lay eggs. These beds are found at depths from a few inches to several feet, and they are almost always close to shore.

Locating beds is easy. You can see the depressions in clear

water where the males have staked out their territory along sandy bottoms. Alert fishermen may also notice disturbances on the surface as busy bluegills dash about, cutting the surface with their dorsal fins.

Serious bluegill fishermen, however, rely more on the sense of smell than on the sense of sight when locating bedding fish. They literally "sniff them out." An active bluegill bed sends forth a distinctive, fishy aroma.

In larger bodies of water, bluegills prefer secluded breeding grounds. They like coves off the main body of the lake, areas where there is plenty of overhanging brush and "stump grounds."

You will seldom find bluegills bedding more than 2 to 3 feet deep (except in cold, clear lakes or where water levels continually fluctuate). They prefer flats or gently sloping banks with sandy bottoms.

Once a bed is located, cast to the perimeter of bedding activity, working inward as you catch fish. This helps avoid disturbing the fish near the center. You can usually catch several bluegills from a single bed, especially if it's a good-sized one. Tandem-rig doubles are common for fishing beds.

When fishing bedding bream, it is ideal to know the location of several beds. When action slows or ceases in one bed, you can move to the next one. Unless conditions change dramatically, bream bed in the same location year after year. The fish on any specific bed will usually be of the same size class, too. If a bed produces nice-sized bluegills—those weighing 3/4 pound or more— you should remember its exact location!

Catching bedding bluegills is easy. Bluegills strike readily at dusk on summer evenings. Surface activity usually happens between spring and Indian summer when insects are available on top. Bluegills can be caught on fly rods, however, any time conditions allow fishing.

Anglers fishing for bluegills in cool and cold weather use nymphs, tiny streamers or wet flies. They sometimes need a sink-tip line or a small split shot or two to get their presentation down to the fish. Bluegills concentrate around structure that offers refuge from their mortal enemy—the bass. Some examples of this structure are the edges of submerged weedbeds, stumps and logs, the edges of docks and piers or even brush piles.

Your fishing tactics will need to be somewhat different from those used in warm months. *Slow* is still a key word; however, you do not leave your fly stationary as you would on the surface. When working nymphs or wet flies, use a steady yet sluggish retrieve. A finger-twist retrieve is ideal. If using streamers, slow, brief twitches work well. Set the hook anytime something seems wrong—cold-weather strikes are very subtle. The metabolism of the fish slows as the water cools; therefore, everything else—from feeding habits to the nature of the take—also slows.

Crappie Methods

Crappies are popular gamefish across the country, and they have several local names, such as sac au lait, speckled perch, slabs and papermouths. Even though crappies lack the spunk of their cousin, the bluegill, they can put up a fight when you're using the proper equipment, such as a 4-weight rod or smaller. Like bluegills, they are plentiful in many waters, and they respond well to fly-rod offerings.

Crappies lack popularity with fly fishermen because most anglers do not realize the crappie's responsiveness. The main item in the crappie diet is minnows. Properly worked streamers should produce numerous strikes when casting to spots holding these fish. Crappies are notorious for schooling; if you catch one, you should catch another.

Crappies love brush piles and other "hides," so hang-ups are common. If you know the exact location of underwater brush piles (and crappie fishermen often do), work your fly only on the edges. Using weed-free streamers and heavy monofilament that protects the hook's bend also helps.

You will seldom tear a fly loose from a crappie's mouth. This is one distinct advantage the fly fisherman has over the angler using conventional tackle. The greater length and added "give" of the fly rod decreases the chances of pulling the hook out of its tender mouth. Fly rods are also more sensitive than standard "hardware."

Although most crappie fishing takes place beneath the surface, there is one time of year you can get some surface action. Like bluegills, crappies spawn in shallow-water beds, and they do not like insects or other small creatures invading their territory. Crappies, therefore, often hit small popping bugs on the surface during the spawning period.

Jigs—second only to minnows—catch crappies. Their dead

Spawning crappies provide fishermen with hefty stringers to take home. Fly fishing for crappies is a fun and rewarding experience.

Starting With Panfish

This "redeye" (rock bass) hit a tiny jig worked with a fly rod. Jig fishing with a fly rod is an ideal method for detecting delicate panfish strikes.

weight makes casting difficult, except with small-sized jigs. However, it is simple to drop a jig over the boat's edge and execute the "jigging" action (up and down). A fly rod does this beautifully, and there is no better tool for detecting strikes from this species. (You can even use the fly rod to dunk minnows for crappies.)

Crappie fishing has its own special appeal, especially the potential platter of hot fillets flanked with coleslaw and hushpuppies. Learning to detect crappie strikes consistently will help prepare you for nymph-fishing more challenging prey, such as trout.

Other Sunfish

There are many other members of the sunfish family that are attractive to the fly fisherman. Pumpkinseeds, longears, shellcrackers, warmouths, stumpknockers, redbreasts and green sunfish are some examples. All have spawning habits similar to bluegills. They are usually at their brightest (color-wise) during the bedding period. The males, who prepare the nests and guard the eggs, are also easily caught at this time. Bluegill fishing techniques work well on most other sunfish. Some species, notably shellcrackers and warmouths, do less surface-feeding than bluegills.

The rock bass, or redeye bass, deserves special attention. Preferring clear, cold water, the rock bass is often found in the same streams as trout or smallmouth bass, although it can live in waters that are too warm for these species. Redeyes usually eat insects; however, they also feed on minnows, insect larvae and small crustaceans. Rock bass strike hard and willingly, and they really fight for a few seconds after being hooked. They are schooling fish that prefer deep, comparatively still holes in streams.

Although it is not a true panfish from a scientific standpoint, the yellow perch, also known as the 'coon perch or ringed perch, is similar in size to most panfish. Yellow perch are found primarily in lakes, and they also are a schooling species. They eat insects, grubs, small minnows and crayfish. Perch are easily caught underwater, so a full sinking line is necessary. Most perch, especially larger ones, are found deep, and streamers work best. More streamlined than sunfish, perch do not have broad bodies to offer resistance when hooked; however, they are good eating.

Panfish are an ideal quarry for the novice fly fisherman because they are easy to catch, provide the chance to "tune up" before fishing other species and offer pure fishing pleasure.

=12=

Trout And Salmon

Trout and salmon are the premier species for fly fishing enthusiasts. There are many reasons for their enduring appeal. For one, they dwell in the most beautiful parts of the country because they require clean, cold waters. Therefore, they are most frequently found in idyllic settings that show little evidence of human developments.

Trout and salmon thrive in various types of water, including beaver ponds, lakes, tailwaters, tiny streams and mighty rivers. The waters must be free of pollution, and they cannot be too turbid. Even though they seem fragile, trout and salmon are surprisingly widespread. The combination of extensive stocking programs and habitat creation in previously unsuitable areas (mainly tailwaters) has helped the trout species grow past its original geographical confines.

Trout and salmon take flies readily. If you add their colorful, streamlined beauty, solid fighting powers and often spectacular, graceful leaping abilities, you realize why these fish are so popular with fly fishermen. Knowing and understanding the various types of water that hold these particular fish species is a major part of fly-fishing success.

Ponds And Small Lakes

Trout can thrive in small bodies of still water in northern climates. Salmonids (the trout and salmon species) do not like warm

Trout and salmon are found in beautiful, scenic waters. Most waters, such as this Western stream, are located in pollution-free environments with little human development.

Trout And Salmon

water temperatures; they cannot survive in still water that becomes too hot during the summer. They also require water that is reasonably well-oxygenated and not overly acidic. Acid rain has caused problems for trout in some Appalachian streams.

If lakes or ponds freeze solid in winter, trout cannot use them—no matter how suitable they are in warmer months. You will, however, find numerous stock ponds and alpine lakes in the West; beaver ponds in New York, New England and the upper Midwest; and several small lakes across the northern United States and Canada that hold trout. Brook trout, in particular, seem to thrive in this still water; rainbow trout grow tremendously fast in some Western ponds.

Feeder springs or submerged springs in still water are advantageous. Small streams that enter and exit beaver ponds are productive, too. These feeder springs and streams act as nurseries for insects, especially if aquatic vegetation is present.

The angler, however, may experience difficulties fishing these waters. Trout that inhabit small, still water bodies tend to spook quite easily. Approaching them within reasonable casting distance without profiling yourself against the skyline can be difficult. Wading also causes problems because the fish are at depths well over the angler's head. Float tubes are an ideal solution, especially in ponds that have more than an acre or two of surface area. In beaver ponds, it is sometimes possible to use the dam as a screen; the angler creeps up from below it and cautiously casts into the still water. Fishing from shore is also an option; however, this fishing method may require considerable stealth, roll casting ability and other special skills.

Small Streams

Small streams which are 30 to 40 feet wide and can be easily waded present no real casting-distance problems. They are much easier to "read" than either large rivers or still water. Fly fishing streams usually entails working upstream while covering the water with dry flies; traditional nymphers and wet-fly fishermen wade downstream. Many modern anglers, however, wade upstream no matter what type of fly they use. Because trout (and salmon too, if in streams this size) face the current's flow, casting from behind them helps prevent you from being spotted. On the other hand, some anglers say that the gravel and vegetation they stir up while

Although it requires special skills, trout fishing from shore can be quite productive in small lakes. If anglers employ stealth, they will most likely catch fish.

working their way downstream cause fish to feed.

There are arguments supporting both upstream and downstream wading, and fly-fishing veterans will use both approaches, depending upon conditions. In small streams where shallow water and short distances have a tendency to reveal the angler's presence more, upstream movement is preferable—even when you need to cast across or down.

Small streams do not usually hold lunker fish; however, the small jewels they provide have their own special rewards. (Small streams offer a sense of "oneness" with your prey, and nowhere are the rhythms of water more beautiful than in an impatient, tumbling freestone creek.) A tiny brook that you could step across may be home to trout. A 7-incher taken in such a brook is as much a trophy as a 7-pounder landed in big water!

Most trout streams are free-flowing. They build up over the course of draining due to myriad feeder springs, seepages and other tiny tributaries. These are usually referred to as freestone creeks. Another small stream encountered less frequently by fly fishermen is a spring creek. Spring creeks evolve from a single large spring underground. These creeks can be found in areas with extensive limestone deposits and aquifers underground. The dissolved limestone provides incredibly rich nutrients for spring creeks. Because the water has cool, consistent temperatures, fish feed in these creeks year-round.

Spring creeks are a true bonanza for trout. They can hold an awesome number of fish. Their weed-filled waters provide not only great quantities of food but superb cover. This is why some spring creeks, such as the Letort in Pennsylvania, are internationally famous.

Big Rivers

Large rivers present special problems in getting the fly into the strike zone. Most are associated with distance; however, anglers also have trouble getting streamers or nymphs to the correct depth in powerful, fast-flowing currents. Those same currents make wading difficult or even dangerous. If anglers are not familiar with a particular stream, they may have trouble determining prime holding spots.

Mighty rivers, however, have several benefits. They are seasonal homes to many salmon and steelhead, and fish size increases with the stream size. Big, brawling rivers have attracted many fly fishermen. These rivers, however, are not good for beginners because they generally demand exceptional skills (some Alaskan waterways are an exception).

Wading is the primary approach in these large rivers. Anglers are now beginning to use MacKenzie boats or similar craft to cover more water. Casting from these boats is easy, and they can be pulled into the shallows or beached when you reach a promising riffle or run. These craft are commonly used on Western rivers. If a newcomer wants to be introduced to big water, a guide with local knowledge and a MacKenzie boat is the solution.

Tailwaters

Literally hundreds of miles of prime trout water, as well as

Tailwater trout tend to grow fast because the water is rich in nutrients. This nice brown trout was caught in Tennessee's Hiwassee River tailrace.

countless acres of land, have been inundated in the name of progress, flood control and hydroelectric power. There has, however, been an unexpected and unintended benefit to the construction of these dams. In many cases, their outflow has produced several miles of marvelous fishing, and, in some parts of the country, it has created habitat suitable for trout where none existed.

Tailwaters, which are created when water comes from the depths of the lake upstream, are plenty cold. They also are rich in nutrients. The world-record brown trout came from an Arkansas tailrace, and many of America's best-known trout streams are tailwaters. These rivers include the Bighorn and Missouri in the West; the White River and North Fork in the heart of the country; and the Clinch, Smith and Nantahala in the Southeast.

Tailraces are raging, roaring rivers that are virtually unwadable when the turbines upstream are turning; however, they become placid, slow-moving streams when the gates are closed. This presents two very different fishing scenarios and thus requires two different tactics.

Most fly fishermen concentrate on tailwaters when the water is "off" (when the dam's turbines are not turning), although fish feed just as much and are not as spooky when the water is "on."

Large Lakes

Big lakes present big problems for trout and salmon fishermen; it is extremely difficult to locate fish. Various trout species thrive in lakes, and landlocked salmon are often found, too. Salmon have been stocked successfully in the Great Lakes. Even lake trout, which are not generally thought of as a suitable fly-fishing quarry, can be taken in shallow waters just after ice-out occurs in the spring.

When fishing large bodies of water, you will find that rise forms are a major indicator of fish location. Whether on shore, wading or fishing from a boat, you should always pay attention to feeding-activity signs. If a lake lacks indicators, you should fish where streams enter or leave the lake. Even an inflow as small as a spring seepage can be productive.

Even though wading or fishing from shore can be successful in large bodies of still water, a float tube, canoe or conventional water craft is a better approach. You can cover more water and backcast freely. Do not, however, venture too far from shore in a belly boat or canoe.

The Species Of Trout

Brook Trout. Although commonly called brook trout or speckled trout, this species is really a member of the char family. Brookies are close cousins of the trout and have the basic habit and habitat characteristics of trout; therefore, they will be considered a trout in this book.

The brook trout is the easiest trout to catch. Small brookies, in particular, attack flies with a vengeance immediately after the fly hits the water. In this regard, the brookie may be its own worst enemy; it is too easily caught. Brook trout are the least tolerant of water temperature, pollution and siltation. In other words, brook trout do not like humans. This is one reason why brookies have all

When fishing large bodies of still water, float tubing is the best approach. Float tubes allow anglers to cover lots of water and cast freely. This 20-inch rainbow shows that anglers can be successful from belly boats.

Trout And Salmon   145

Even a tiny brook trout can be a prize on a tiny stream high up in the Appalachian chain. Although brook trout are easily caught, they are the least tolerant of human presence.

but disappeared over much of their original range, especially in the Eastern United States. As deforestation progressed, brook trout numbers and their home waters dwindled. Brook trout also do not compete well with other trout species in some parts of the country. In the southern Appalachians, for example, the introduction of rainbow trout drove the native brook trout to headwater streams and tributaries. Today, brook trout are endangered in the Great Smoky Mountains National Park, a region where they once thrived.

Brook trout populations have been decreasing over the years, especially in the eastern part of the country. Anglers who want world-class brook-trout fishing must be willing to travel to remote regions. The world's finest brook-trout fisheries are in out-of-the-way places like the Minipi River in Labrador and virtually unfished Canadian streams.

High up along the spine of the Appalachians, in beaver ponds and brooks in the upper Midwest and over much of the West, brook trout remain plentiful. In fact, they will overpopulate in certain situations. They are beautiful fish, especially when they put on their brilliant spawning colors in the fall.

Brookies like bright objects. Attractor patterns with red, white or yellow colors in them, such as a Royal Wulff or Yellow Humpy, work well on the surface. Beneath the surface, a Mickey Finn or tinsel-laden nymph is best. Most brook trout are found in smaller streams, beaver ponds or alpine lakes.

Brook trout stay in a stream's still water; they do not like to fight the main current. The lower end of long runs, the edge of riffles, backwaters or places with still pockets behind in-stream obstructions, such as a log or boulder, are all likely holding spots. Brookies also tend to hit flies that are "danced" on the water or fished like living insects.

Rainbow Trout. The rainbow trout, with its vivid lateral stripe of red and aerial acrobatics, is the favorite trout of most fly fishermen. Rainbows live in various waters, including their natural-habitat waters and those in which they were stocked. Rainbows are found across the United States in areas with the right climatic conditions and suitable waters.

Although quite adaptable and satisfied in everything from high-country ponds to spring creeks, rainbows are the premier species in fast-flowing, rock-laden streams. Brown trout and, to a

Rainbow trout have glorious colors and execute fantastic aerial acrobatics. Large rainbows, like this 18-incher, will hit minnow-imitating patterns such as the Muddler Minnow.

lesser extent, brookies avoid fast currents, favoring more energy-efficient holding spots. Rainbows, on the other hand, can be found in the middle of the fastest part of the stream. The only thing they need is a small rock or pocket for holding.

Rainbows are great surface feeders—even when they reach large sizes. If there is some hatch activity, you will most likely find rainbows on the surface. They will take various insect patterns readily; larger rainbows will also hit patterns imitating minnows, crayfish and other food items. When there are no hatches, rainbows feed eclectically, and they are not bothered by bright sunlight. When compared to brown trout, for example, rainbows can be taken more easily during the day's middle hours—even when the sky is clear overhead.

Once hooked, rainbows will fight until they're exhausted; they execute one water-clearing leap after another with their gills flaring and red sides shining in the sun. There is no trout more beautiful than a flamboyantly colored rainbow.

Steelhead. Steelhead trout are rainbows that live in saltwater or big freshwater lakes and enter streams during the spawning season. Even though they are the same fish species, they vary strikingly from rainbows that spend their entire lives in streams. Steelhead are metallic silver in color and grow to impressive sizes, dwarfing most of their rainbow brethren.

Like salmon, steelhead return to spawn in the river in which they were born. The timing of this "run" varies considerably. Late fall is the most common time for runs; however, they may occur in spring or winter. Some rivers have more than one run annually.

Steelhead usually hit out of irritation or reflex—not hunger (they do not feed during the spawning migration). Brightly colored flies work best when fishing them. Most steelhead are caught well beneath the surface, so you will need to use sinking line to get your streamer to the proper depth. Most steelhead rivers are deep, powerful streams that require fast-sinking lines.

Casting to steelhead entails quartering upstream, then mending line to get the fly down deep as quickly as possible. Steelhead fishing also involves the use of "searching" casts when you need to cover a lot of water. The water should be covered methodically—cast and allow the fly to drift through the pool, then take two or three steps and cast again.

Steelhead move upstream to spawn; they congregate to rest

This big cutthroat came fresh from a spawning run out of Yellowstone Lake. Cutthroats resemble rainbows, except for the colorful slash across the throat.

during the journey below particularly rough stretches of water or places where the stream drops rapidly. Anglers should focus on these "stacked" steelhead. (Steelhead can also be found resting directly above obstacles.)

Steelhead fishing requires patience and arm strength! You need to use a heavy rod (at least 8-weight) and make lengthy casts. When you finally hook one of these silver streaks, all the aches and pains will be forgotten.

Cutthroat Trout. Cutthroat trout, or "cutts," are widespread in the West. They get their name from the distinct reddish-orange slash that cuts across the gill plates, or throat. Aside from this characteristic, cutthroats resemble rainbows, and they often cross-breed if living in the same waters. The resulting hybrid species is described as a "cutbow."

Second only to brookies, cutthroat are the easiest trout to catch, especially in places with little fishing pressure. (Heavily fished catch-and-release streams, such as Slough Creek in Yellowstone National Park, can be a major cutthroat-catching challenge.) If fishing in remote alpine lakes in the Rockies or in small streams at 6,000 to 7,000 feet, you will most likely get a strike on every cast. Cutts prefer dry flies; however, flashy streamers work best in streams clouded from snow melt or sudden summer showers. In meandering streams that flow slowly through upland meadows, nymphs attract strikes when dry flies are consistently rejected.

Cutts, like rainbows, are frequently found in the heart of the stream. They also prefer undercut banks and deep eddies found in streams swollen by heavy spring runoffs.

Brown Trout. An import from Europe, the brown trout is the wiliest and wariest member of the trout family. Browns are rather reclusive; you will rarely find them feeding in bright sunlight. Browns prefer low-light conditions. Dawn and dusk are usually the most productive times to fish for browns, especially in small streams. During the summer, this is somewhat true for all trout. During twilight hours, evenings in particular, heavy insect hatches often occur which spark the feeding activity.

Brown trout feed heavily on insects. As they grow in size, browns become nocturnal in their habits and selective in their diet. Supremely energy efficient, big browns like big bites. After reaching a foot in length, they eat fewer flies and turn instead to minnows, small trout and sculpins. If you want to hook a really big brown on a fly, use a streamer.

A heavy hatch (especially large-insect hatches, such as stoneflies) persuades browns of all sizes to feed—no matter what time of day. A "grasshopper wind" that sweeps across open meadows on a summer's day pushing hordes of hoppers into a stream also causes browns to go on a binge.

For the most part, however, it takes artful casting and knowledge of preferred lies to catch these wary warriors. You will seldom find browns in the main flow of the stream. Instead, they hold in convenient ambush posts, such as the underside of logs, behind rocks and beneath crumbling banks. If you find a deep eddy or a smooth pocket directly above a place where two riffles run together, you have most likely found a brown.

These lies present a problem. They are difficult to cast to, and they prevent anglers from getting a decent dry-fly float. It is also difficult to "see" dry flies in low-light periods when browns feed. These low-light conditions also make it difficult to land the brown after it's hooked. Heavy browns tend to sulk on the bottom or beneath rocks.

Brown trout prefer lies such as deep eddies. They feed mostly on insects; however, they eat minnows, small trout and sculpin after reaching about a foot in length.

If night-fishing for trout is legal in your area, it is a great way to take big browns. They roam freely where they would not venture during the day. If you hook a really nice brown and it refuses to budge from the bottom, jarring the butt of your rod with metal, such as the back of your pocket-knife blade or your hemostats, will sometimes make the fish move.

Other Trout. There are other trout species that can be caught with flies. Lake trout, for example, are a popular gamefish; however, they usually hold too deep in lakes for fly-fishing methods.

Dolly Varden trout, also known as bull trout, are actually from the char family. Natives of the Pacific slope, Dolly Vardens are found primarily in Canada and Alaska. They feed voraciously and can be caught easily if abundant. They do not fight as well as other trout, but they are delicious eating.

Golden trout are not found throughout the country. Originally found only in California's Volcano Creek, goldens have been successfully transplanted and are now moderately widespread in Western creeks and lakes. They thrive only in high altitudes; thus, golden-trout fishing requires long hikes.

Most other trout species, such as the Sunapee (or Eastern golden trout) and the marble trout of Yugoslavia are either so rare or so inaccessible that they never seem to enter the average angler's fishing plans.

The arctic grayling and the arctic char are not trout species, but they should be mentioned. Both are found in the far North— in northern Canada or Alaska. There is also a Montana grayling species, but it is in trouble because of its required habitat of unpolluted waters.

Both char and grayling hit flies readily. Arctic char grow to double-digit weights in the limited areas where they are abundant. Grayling, on the other hand, rarely weigh over 2 pounds.

Salmon

Atlantic Salmon. The Atlantic salmon is the king of fly fishing. No species is more fabled in literature than these supremely beautiful fish. Catching Atlantic salmon is not that difficult if you are in a location where they are abundant. They will take flies when the mood strikes them; however, they sometimes ignore any and all offerings for hours.

Atlantic salmon have suffered mightily from commercial fishing—the species is in trouble. Decades ago, pollution drove them away from their New England range, although valiant conservation efforts are resulting in signs of a salmon comeback. Atlantic-salmon fishing is limited to a few rivers on the Canadian seaboard, Iceland, the British Isles and the Scandinavian countries. Choice "beats" (water stretches reserved for an individual's exclusive use on a given day) on fine salmon rivers are coveted and costly. (Anyone who plans to do much fishing for Atlantic salmon needs to have a substantial bank account.)

Unlike the various Pacific salmon, Atlantic salmon survive spawning and may return two or more times to lay eggs. The yearling salmon are known as "grilse." The spawning run takes place during warm months. It can begin as early as May or as late as early autumn, depending upon location.

Atlantic salmon are royalty when it comes to fly fishing; they leap repeatedly once hooked. An assortment of bright wet flies and streamers is your best bet when fishing this species.

Brightly dressed wet flies are commonly used to take Atlantic salmon. Casts are made across the current, allowing the line to swing downstream. The ideal drift carries the fly along a few inches under the surface; keep the line tight and slack-free at all times. Atlantic salmon take flies leisurely. Strikes usually come so close to the surface that you "see" the take before you feel the fish! Many fly fishermen set the hook too quickly when they first fish Atlantic salmon; this takes the fly away from the fish. Experienced hands wait until the salmon turns its head toward the bottom or until its weight can be felt on the line.

Once hooked, Atlantic salmon leap repeatedly. They are, along with tarpon, the most acrobatic species caught on a fly.

Pacific Salmon. While there is only one species of Atlantic salmon, there are several Pacific-salmon species. Pacific salmon are caught during their spawning runs because they die after they spawn. Fly fishermen catch them when they're fresh from the sea. Pacific salmon become weaker as they travel upstream. When these fish first arrive from the sea, they still have their bright silver coloration from saltwater. As the spawning run progresses, they begin to develop red hues. Pacific salmon can be confusing because there are several species, and each species has two or more names: king (or chinook), silver (or coho), humpback (or pink), chum (or dog salmon) and sockeye (or blueback). The king and silver salmon are the most popular fly-fishing species.

Once salmon enter freshwater, their only priority is to spawn. When strikes occur, they are merely incidental to movement upstream. A fly stripped in front of them, however, will often draw strikes. This is because it is either an irritant or a trigger to a feeding reflex from its saltwater days. While wet flies are common for Atlantic-salmon fishing, streamers are popular for Pacific-salmon fishing. Egg or egg-and-sperm patterns, such as the Babine family, are widely used. Those featuring gold or silver tinsel, such as the Christmas Tree, also attract strikes.

Alaska has the finest Pacific-salmon fishing, although Canada has some productive waters, too. Salmon fishing has dramatically declined in the West Coast states. This is the result of pollution, dams, inadequate fish ladders, destruction of spawning grounds, too much commercial fishing and other harmful practices. There are, however, plenty of healthy Pacific-salmon fisheries for the angler seeking action. Pacific-salmon fishing is preferable to the quest for the Atlantic species because there are more Pacific-salmon fisheries and species.

The various Pacific-salmon species have different migration times, spreading the fishing season out over four months or so. Other marvelous fly-rod quarries tag along as the salmon migrate, feasting madly on their eggs. These include rainbow trout, grayling, Dolly Vardens and arctic char. In clear water, you can sometimes see these fish bumping the stomachs of roe-laden hen salmon in an effort to knock eggs loose.

King salmon are the first of the Pacific species to migrate, and they are a real fly-rod prize because of their great size. Hooking a fish fresh from the sea in the 30-pound (or larger) range is a tremendous thrill, and the average king will usually weigh well over 20 pounds.

Silver salmon enter freshwater later in the year than kings—usually in late July or early August. They hit flies more readily than other Pacific-salmon species. Silvers also do a lot of jumping—even after they've journeyed hundreds of miles.

No matter which Pacific-salmon species you're fishing, quartering casts with short strips work well. Drifts that do not strip also are effective; the current and the line's belly carry the fly. A high percentage of strikes will happen when the fly begins to straighten out at the end of the drift.

Landlocked Salmon. Landlocked salmon are similar to Atlantic salmon except for size. They have been successfully stocked in several fisheries and are found in New York, throughout New England and in Canada's Maritime Provinces. Landlocked salmon have also been introduced in the Great Lakes. Landlocked salmon hit flies quite readily; however, there are only two times during the year that they can be found in depths suitable for fly fishing. They travel to shallow water after the ice melts in the spring, and they move into the running water of feeder streams to spawn in October. If there are no feeder streams, they spawn in the lake.

Landlocks eat various foods, including insects. Their favorite food, however, is smelt. Streamers are the most productive fly-fishing pattern. Most fly fishing is done during warm months, and trolling with lead-core line gets the fly down deep. This isn't the typical fly-fishing technique of "cast and catch," but it's about the only way to take landlocked salmon on a fly during hot weather.

Another landlocked salmon, at least in the sense that it never leaves freshwater, is the kokanee. Kokanee are found primarily in the West, although they have been successfully stocked in at least one Southern reservoir (North Carolina's Lake Aquone). Kokanee feed on microorganisms so they are difficult to catch on a fly. The best time to fly fish for kokanee is during their annual spawning run into moving water.

=13=

Going After Bass

Tackle and techniques have changed for bass fishing over the years, but a properly fished bug still drives bass crazy. In fact, it may be the fish-catchingest bass lure around! Today's fishermen have become so enthralled with big boats, fancy state-of-the-art gear, depthfinders and exotic lures that the devoted bass bugger (which encompasses all types of bass fly fishing) and his craft are overlooked.

Bugs position the lure in a way that draws almost constant strikes. Fly fishermen do not need to reel in line before casting; the bug is simply cast into and worked through the potential striking zone, lifted and cast again.

Bug fishing also covers more types of water and is more quiet than any other method. A bass bug—even a heavy one made from deer hair tied on a 1/0 or 2/0 hook—lands on the water like a feather compared to a plug, which splashes down. The loud "ker-plunk" of a weighty lure often sends heavily pressured bass quickly to cover.

A fly rod enables you to cast a bug into many of the so-called "impossible places." Submerged vegetation is not a problem when using a floating bug and line; however, a knotless leader is needed if the vegetation extends to the surface. Stick-ups simply challenge casting skills, and overhanging limbs pose few problems when roll casting. The adept bug fisherman can even work in water that lacks backcasting space. Fishing from a canoe, johnboat or float tube allows you to quietly cover the water.

Bass bugging is a favorite method among fly fishermen because it drives bass crazy! This smallmouth bass smashes an attractive popper pattern.

Going After Bass

Once you catch your first decent bass on a bug, you will most likely be hooked for life. There are few things that compare with a smashing surface strike from a bass that inhales a bug.

Equipment

Your bass-fishing outfit will somewhat depend upon your selected quarry. Most situations, however, will require at least a 7-weight rod. Many bass fishermen prefer 8- or 9-weights. (For powerful stripers, you will need an outfit similar to one used in saltwater flats fishing.) The rod should have a lot of backbone to turn over wind-resistant flies and set the hook with authority. It should also be fairly stiff. Longer rods are best, especially if casting from a seated position in a canoe or float tube.

A matching line with a conventional weight-forward taper should be used, although a bug taper (a heavier, shorter taper) also works. The bug taper enables a caster to properly turn over big, wind-resistant bugs and streamers. Floating lines work best in most bass-fishing conditions; sink-tip lines are advantageous when fishing streamers in moving water.

A 7- to 9-foot tapered leader works best, and the tippet should be fairly strong—6- or even 8-pound test will suffice. When fishing spooky bass in shallow-water conditions, such as late-summer smallmouth fishing in streams, a longer leader and lighter tippet are advisable. Bass usually are not leader shy. The type of fly or bug you're using will somewhat determine your leader needs. A fine, flexible tippet, for example, will not turn over a big streamer or bulky bug, such as a deer-hair mouse.

The bugs and flies used for bass are not required to have the amount of detail that bugs and flies used for other fish like trout need. Largemouths, in particular, will hit almost anything if they're in the mood. You should, however, be aware of the primary food items in the water you are fishing. Casting Muddler Minnows in a stream where crayfish are the main diet item, for example, will reduce your chances of getting strikes.

There are many fly and bug patterns available to fly fishermen. Having a selection of sliders, poppers and streamers in various sizes and colors is beneficial.

Where To Find Bass

Bass can be found throughout most of the country. They are

Southern farm ponds, such as this one in southern Georgia, can hold lunker largemouths. Fly fishermen enjoy fishing ponds from shore, docks or belly boats.

America's most popular gamefish. Fly fishermen are really not threatened by the angling competition. There are countless farm ponds and private lakes that encompass hundreds of acres—and bass! Bass in moving water are also often overlooked by the "run and gun" fellows in the big boats. In smaller streams, these craft are prohibited. Even on larger reservoirs with heavy fishing pressure, few will be using a fly rod.

Streams primarily hold smallmouth bass, but largemouths can be found in the current. If possible, stripers may even move into the larger rivers during their spawning period. For small, fast-flowing streams, wading is the best fly-fishing approach. In larger rivers, a canoe or johnboat works best.

If fishing for bass in moving waters, look for potential holding spots. These would be places where there is a break in the current:

Going After Bass

Fly fisherman Brian Donahue works likely smallmouth water in New York. Smallmouths are found throughout much of the country and thrive in cool, rumbling streams.

eddies, deep pools, undercut banks and certain rock or log placements. Largemouth bass do not like really fast-flowing waters; smallmouths thrive in streams that tumble and rumble.

Largemouth bass live in waters that have suitable oxygen levels and temperatures. Bass thrive in most farm ponds; they cannot survive in ponds that freeze solid in winter. In the South, a small, one-acre pond could be home to behemoth largemouths weighing up to 10 pounds or more! Ponds are ideal for fly fishermen; they are usually shallow, offer plenty of visible structure and seldom have barren sections where there are absolutely no fish.

When fishing ponds, you can cover most of the water from shore. You can also stalk fish in a float tube when you see a disturbance or sign. This useful watercraft lets you cover every inch of the pond.

Bass location within the pond will vary depending upon the season. During spring and fall, bass are in the shallows and around cover like weedbeds and stumps. In summer, fish will most likely be in deeper areas near dams or around submerged springs, although they may move into the shallows to feed on insects, frogs and tadpoles during the cooler morning and evening hours.

Vast portions of deep lakes are beyond the scope of fly-fishing equipment and techniques. It would be impractical to fly fish for bass suspended at 40 feet. Fly fishermen can, however, score bass in some areas of big lakes. Understanding the limitations (and advantages) of equipment, considering the habits and habitat of bass and fishing accordingly contribute to fly-fishing success.

Spring and fall are the best seasons to fly fish for largemouths on most reservoirs. Water temperatures at depths of 1 to 5 feet are acceptable to the fish, and, more importantly, bass can find an abundance of food in the shallows. May and September are "magic" months for bass fishing across the country. In May, bass are voracious after spawning. In September, bass "stock up" on food, preparing for winter. During summer months, fly fishermen should focus on areas around cover close to deep water: Shoreline riprap, banks that have sharp drop-offs, in-water structure and docks are all good places to find bass. At dawn or dusk, fish move into areas where small branches or creeks enter the lake.

The Beauty Of Bronzebacks
Smallmouth bass, or bronzebacks, are a great quarry for the fly fisherman. Powerful, highly acrobatic fish, smallmouths can bore for the bottom one instant and be airborne the next. Smallmouths are abundant in streams, as well as lakes with sufficiently clean and cool water. No matter what type of water body they live in, they always concentrate around rocks.

Approaches for taking smallmouths in streams and for taking them in lakes are quite similar. Successful topwater tactics include various dry flies imitating caddis flies, stone flies and damselflies. Skaters, flies with oversized hackle that are bounced and skittered across the surface, also work well. Terrestrial imitators, especially grasshopper and cricket patterns, are excellent choices for small-mouths from midsummer into the fall. These patterns need to be large—tied on No. 6 to 8 hooks—to attract interest from big smallmouths.

Dry flies can be dead-drifted, which allows them to float with the current; however, imparting some action usually is better. If a smallmouth has a specific feeding station during a heavy insect hatch, a drag-free float will most likely attract the fish.

Medium-sized poppers are also a standard, topwater small-mouth bait. They come in various shapes, sizes and colors. Among

Smallmouth bass are abundant in streams and can also be found in lakes with cool, clean water. These smallmouths were found near rocks in a fast-moving stream.

the best of them are Darter Bugs, the Skipping Bugs designed by Bill Gallasch, Sneaky Petes (a slider-type bug), Dahlberg Divers, deer-hair mice and frog imitators and Tapply's Bass Bug (a flat-faced deer-hair bug). Most bugs are more effective with some action imparted to them. Short strips or gentle jerks are usually recommended, although sometimes audible "poppings" are required to attract strikes.

Smallmouths respond well to streamers and nymphs, too. Hellgrammites (dobsonfly larvae) are a significant portion of the smallmouth's diet in many streams, and the Murray Hellgrammite is a deadly smallmouth fly. Although hellgrammites can move through the water quite rapidly, you should fish the Murray Hellgrammite pattern on the bottom where hellgrammites live. Other useful nymph patterns are the Bitch Creek nymph and

Brooks' Dark Stone Fly Nymph. Smaller nymphs commonly used for trout often work well, too.

Crayfish, lizards and leeches are all popular smallmouth food items. Patterns imitating these creatures have become more readily available in recent years. Minnows are probably the most important food source for smallmouths. There are more streamer patterns imitating minnows than any other food item. Some recommended patterns include Shenk's Sculpin, the Spuddler (a cross between a standard streamer and a Muddler Minnow) and Whitlock's Sculpin. Another pattern, the Strymph, involves an unusual approach. It is a hybrid—a cross between a dragonfly nymph and a streamer—that is fished somewhat the same way as a jig. It is cast upstream in moving water. The fly "bounces" along the stream's bottom on a tight line while the current carries it toward the angler.

Fly Fishing For Largemouths

Although the best fly-fishing action for smallmouths is in streams, still water is where it's at for largemouths. Wading can still be a viable approach, especially in small ponds or lakes that drop off gradually; however, most fly fishermen use boats when fishing for largemouths. Surface lures—dry flies and poppers—are important for largemouth fishing. This is partly because a lot of shallow-water habitat that largemouths favor is chock full of vegetation and other underwater impediments. If you go beneath the surface, you will definitely need a knotless leader. This will help avoid weeds hanging on the knots. In weedy waters, bugs tied with a loop of stiff monofilament to make the hook snag-free are a real plus. This enables the angler to skitter a surface bug over lily pads, for example, without too much trouble. Smashing strikes are often the result!

When fishing with floating bugs or flies, the biggest problem for beginners and veterans alike is impatience. The longer you can leave the bug still after the cast, the better. Experienced bass buggers sometimes say, "Wait as long as you can stand it, then double that time." You should at least keep the bug motionless until all the disturbance from its landing disappears. Give the bug a twitch, then let it sit again. The twitch should be imparted by moving the line rather than the rod. The rodtip should be low and pointed at the bug at all times. This will give you maximum leverage to set the hook when a fish strikes. There is probably nothing more frustrating than a fish spitting a bug out before hookset because there was too much slack!

Boisterous strikes often happen immediately after the first hint of motion from the bug. It seems like a bass is lying beneath the surface daring its prey to show any sign of life. If nothing happens after the first twitch, let the fly remain motionless for 10 to 15 seconds. Then, you can use one of several types of retrieves: Loud "pops," erratic ones resembling a wounded minnow and fast strips imitating escape all can be effective. In fact, versatility is a hallmark skill of good fly fishermen. You can make a bug pop loudly or softly, gurgle, jump, wiggle, swim or "talk" to bass. If a specific retrieving tactic works consistently, use it almost exclusively as long as it continues to yield strikes.

Bass bugging is a warm-weather sport. Depending upon where you live, this means anything from four to 12 months of fine fishing. Bass bugging produces during the stifling "dog days" of summer when ordinary bass fishing is at its worst. You can fish in daylight and at dusk. On quiet ponds, you can fish at night by sound.

The best surface bug fishing is during the spring and fall. When water temperatures are right, bass that are ravenously hungry roam the shallows.

In selecting flies, choose a few of the more basic bug shapes. Peck's Bad Boy, named after Ernest H. Peckenpaugh, the "father" of American bass bugging, has long been a favorite. Gerbubble Bugs, as well as Desperate Divers, are also consistently effective. Dahlberg Divers (especially those tied with rabbit fur), damselfly imitations, Whitlock Deerhair bugs, Sneaky Petes and Hula Poppers should be included in your bug collection. Even large versions of trout flies will take bass.

Stripers Are Sensational

A select few enjoy fly fishing for striped bass. Stripers are an anadromous species that fisheries biologists have learned how to raise and stock successfully in impoundments with no outlet to the sea. These fish still follow the traditional pattern of leaving their saltwater homes to spawn in freshwater. Wherever found, stripers offer the fly fisherman a tremendous challenge.

Longer casts are needed for striper fishing compared to smallmouth or largemouth fishing. The ability to punch out casts of 70

Striped bass, such as this 12-pounder, offer the fly fisherman an exciting challenge. Big rods (9- or 10-weights) are needed to cast 70 feet or more, and backing is essential.

feet or more is important. This requires using big rods. Nine- or 10-weight rods, which are also used for saltwater species like bonefish, work best. Plenty of backing—at least 100 yards—and a fighting butt are needed. It is also essential to have a reel with a reliable drag because the first run of a 15-pound striper certainly will be a sizzling one!

Catching these powerful fish is a specialized undertaking. You should look for them on the surface, smashing through shad or other minnows. Try getting close enough to cast into the feeding frenzy without spooking the fish. If this is possible, anything that resembles the bait they are chasing will work. (White bass and hybrids also "herd" baitfish to the surface and then gorge on them in this way.)

Whether you pursue stripers or concentrate on largemouths or smallmouths, fly fishing for bass offers great excitement.

=14=

Northerns And Muskies

orthern pike are one of the most voracious and hard-hitting fish in freshwater. If in the mood, they will strike almost any offering that vaguely resembles food. Their close cousin, the muskie, is opposite in its feeding habits. In fact, muskies are known as "the fish of 10,000 casts." Pike, however, can be more selective in their feeding habits at times, and muskies are not impossible to catch. Both species make great quarries for fly fishermen. Catching a trophy-sized fish of either species is rewarding and exciting.

Because of their proportions, preferred habitat and razor-sharp teeth, northerns and muskies can be extremely challenging for fly fishermen; they also present several problems. Most of the problems will pertain to equipment. Anyone who plans to fish either species should be aware of the potential problems and take special care in preparing for the trip. Many pike, as well as muskies, are caught more-or-less by accident.

Pike inhabit some waters containing trout and smallmouth bass. Most anglers who have spent a lot of time fishing these waters have seen a monstrous pike emerge suddenly from a weedbed to inhale a popper or smash a streamer in an area thought to only hold brookies or bronzebacks. When this happens, the fish's sharp teeth usually sever the fragile leader.

Equipment
Leaders. When fishing for northerns or muskies, use a foot or

Northern pike will strike just about any offering when they're in the mood. This youngster took this 9-pound northern on a fly rod, proving once again that fly fishing is for all ages.

Northerns And Muskies

so of shock tippet, which is at least 40-pound-test monofilament, at the end of your leader. You will need strong, special knots to tie the quite disparate sizes of leader together. Behind the shock tippet, you can use whatever pound-test leader you desire. These "water wolves" are not leader shy, so variations in monofilament strength will depend upon things like striving for line-class records, wanting maximum fights out of hooked fish or trying to boat fish as soon as possible.

An alternative to using heavy monofilament as your terminal tackle is using wire—coated or braided. There are problems with using wire, as well as monofilament. Some difficulties associated with wire are tying knots connecting the wire to the hook and turning the fly over on the cast. When casting, you should never use more than what is absolutely necessary. Six inches will suffice in most conditions, and even then the fly lands sloppily.

If an angler catches a record-class fish with the use of a shock tippet, the tippet behind it (which determines the line class) must be at least 15 inches long.

Rods. You will need a powerful rod to turn bigger fish because they will most likely head for cover as soon as they are hooked. A heavy rod with plenty of backbone is also helpful in casting large flies and for hooksetting. Certain parts of northern and muskie mouths are so tough that they seem armor-plated; a rod with extreme hooksetting power is needed. The fly fisherman also should pay a lot of attention to hook sharpness. In fact, the hook and leader should be checked every time a fish is hooked, whether landed or not.

An 8-, 9- or 10-weight rod, which is 8½ to 9 feet long, works best. Distance casting may be important when fishing muskies, and turning over heavy streamers or big-bodied poppers—even in strong winds—may also be a factor in rod selection.

Reels, Backing And Fighting Butts. Floating or sink-tip line is the best choice for muskie and northern-pike fishing; a good reel and ample backing are also necessary. Even though pike thrash wildly on the water's surface or dig down into weedbeds, they can also make sizzling runs when they see a boat. Muskies are exceptionally strong fish with more "staying" power than northerns; a big muskie is capable of a 50- to 75-yard run.

Both species of fish can weigh about 30 pounds and still be a realistic quarry for fly fishermen! A reel with a reliable drag and

A guide hoists a 20-pound-plus pike the author landed on a fly rod. Hooksetting pike, as well as muskies, calls for a powerful rod.

plenty of backing is necessary. A fighting butt is also quite helpful.

Flies. Muskies and pike prefer flies with a lot of flash and bright colors. Streamers made with plenty of flash-abou material seem to attract pike. During the spawning season, which is the best time to fly fish for pike and muskies, pike will hit almost any-thing. Big surface lures work well; however, streamers that are cast tight against weedbeds or brush, then stripped back rapidly are most effective.

Effective Muskie Techniques

Unlike northern pike, muskies can be found in the southern part of the country. They are natives of the Mississippi River drainage, and have been reintroduced to waters that were once considered home. It is now possible to fish for muskies year-round in some states, including North Carolina, Tennessee, Virginia and Kentucky.

During cooler months in the muskie's southern range, streamers work best (this is also true during spring and fall in the northern part of the country). In moving water, muskies can be found in eddies at the edge of deep pools, pockets behind logjams and similar ambush spots. You should cast to the far side of these locations and rapidly strip the streamer back toward you. If this does not provoke action, vary your retrieve by imparting erratic or stop-and-go motion to the streamer. Do not cast "blind" in moving water. Concentrate on the few locations that appear to be tailor-made for muskies.

Fishing for muskies in large bodies of still water can be difficult during cool or cold months because the fish will most likely be at depths beyond fly-fishing techniques. In warm weather, however, muskies are in shallow water close to weedbeds, sunken trees or similar structure. It is possible, at this time, to draw surface strikes with big poppers or flies that imitate crippled minnows. Streamers fished with floating line and worked a foot or two below the top also work.

Admittedly, muskies are tough to catch; however, they will strike big flies with appetizing appearances just as readily as they would plugs or bait. You will most likely get hits from comparatively small fish, but leg-length muskies are possible.

Northern Pike Tactics

Northern pike are quite predictable; they seem to be either hungry or angry most of the time. Thousands of trout fishermen miss opportunities when fishing waters in Alaska and Canada. Brook trout, salmon or grayling are usually the intended quarry of their angling adventure; however, there are probably some majestic northerns in the area, too. Pike usually get no respect; they are cursed for cutting leaders and loathed by guides. On a rainy, overcast day, however, when no insects are hatching and trout are uncooperative, pike can provide some exciting action.

Pike are a spring, summer and early fall quarry for fly fishermen because they are found in the northern part of the country. Pike fishing begins in late spring when pike congregate in shallows to spawn. In lakes, they can be found in protected bays, backwaters and areas with sandy bottoms that are attractive for laying

This pike hit a bright streamer. Pike are especially attracted to yellow or red streamers mixed with some tinsel or flash-abou.

eggs. Flooded brush inundated by spring runoff is a particularly good place.

If you find one pike in any of these locations, you will most likely find others nearby. These can be big fish, too—not the 1- to 4-pound streamlined "hammer handles" encountered as the weather warms. After the lean times of winter, pike in both the pre- and post-spawn mode are exceptionally hungry. They will readily hit bright streamers, especially those that are yellow or red mixed with some tinsel or flash-abou; a big deer-hair mouse will also promote vicious topwater strikes.

As the season progresses, pike become more dispersed. In large lakes, they prefer weedbeds. Minnow-imitating streamers worked alongside or over weedbeds are highly effective, and topwater offerings also attract pike. When fishing weedbeds, you must have open water between you and the weedbed. This keeps the fish from seeking refuge in underwater vegetation. It also reduces the chances of losing fish because of entangling weeds. This approach also works when fishing the pike's summertime hangout—beneath trees that have tumbled into the water or been washed to shore. Pike hold in the shade of these hideaways, waiting for lunch. If

As the weather warms, more 1- to 4-pound "hammer handles" can be found. This hammer-handle pike was taken on a fly rod in the rain.

Complete Angler's Library

one darts out to engulf your fly, avoid cover if possible. Once your hook is set, try to pursue the fight in open water.

Small lakes that range from a few acres to 100 acres often contain only pike, perch and minnows. These lakes are an overlooked yet first-rate fishing resource, and many are perfect for fly fishing. Float tubes can be advantageous in many small-lake situations, especially in places where it would be virtually impossible to fish from even the smallest canoe. The fish may be rather small in these lakes compared to the fish in larger lakes. Occasionally, however, you will fight a double-figure fish of the ax-handle—not hammer-handle—class. Smaller fish are a great challenge on fly-fishing tackle, too.

Pike are also abundant in northern streams. The key to success when fishing in moving water is knowing where to find the fish. Although they may be an ancient fish species, pike are extremely energy efficient. They will not be found fighting the current or in haunts that sap their strength. Plunge-pool edges in deep water, still areas formed by natural "breaks" (like boulders) and eddies are potential holding spots for pike. Pike are an easier prey in streams than in lakes because they are easier to find.

Most pike and muskies have not been the focus of fly-fishing attention. This means that even in heavily fished waters where plugs, spoons and spinners are commonplace, these two species may be naive to fly-fishing offerings. Use this to your advantage.

=15=

Starting In Saltwater

W hether fishing the surf, wading or poling the flats, working tidal marshes and estuaries or concentrating on deep water, there are various saltwater species that will hit flies readily. If you have access to saltwater, you will most likely catch fish on flies. There are some differences between handling a 4-weight outfit and a 9- or 10-weight one. You will, however, be pleased to know that the weight difference is only a few ounces, and, to a considerable degree, the more powerful rods compensate for the bulkier flies you will be using.

Furthermore, modern technology has made saltwater fishing easier. Today, not only are exceptional rods available but there are numerous lines and reels designed specifically with the saltwater fly fisherman in mind.

Equipment

Saltwater fly fishing requires special equipment. The salt air and water can corrode reels, guides, reel seats and hooks that aren't made of noncorroding materials. Along with salt, wind can also be a problem. Because of greater living demands in the saltwater environment, saltwater species are more powerful than freshwater species. This means they put greater strain on tackle.

The well-equipped saltwater fly fisherman can manage with only two rod outfits. A 9-weight and a 12-weight are the best choices. The 9-weight works great in the flats and for most inshore species, while the 12-weight is suitable for tarpon, tuna,

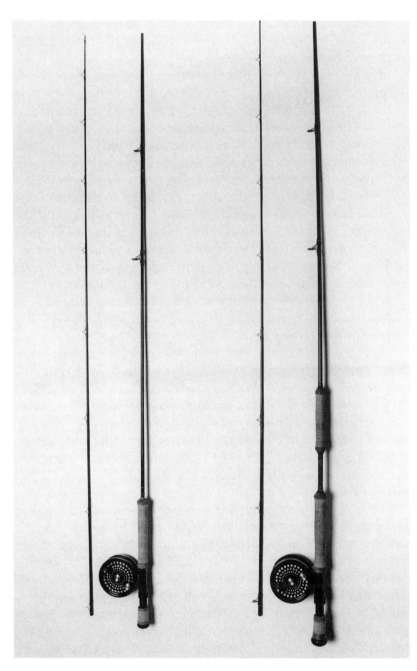

Shown here are two custom-built rod outfits for saltwater fishing. On the left is a 9-weight outfit with an Abel #3N reel and 990 Sage RPL rod. To the right is a 12-weight outfit with an Abel #4 reel and 1220 Sage RPL tarpon rod.

sharks and billfish. If strong winds occur in places where you normally use a 9-weight, the 12-weight gives you the extra "punch" needed in casting a fly.

Because high performance is necessary in saltwater, you should be prepared to spend some extra money acquiring equipment. In the case of rods, this means purchasing graphite, which is today's best rod-making material. Graphite has greater recovery powers than fiberglass and bamboo—two other widely used rod materials. The quality of graphite varies widely, too. Graphite rods that were state-of-the-art as little as five years ago have been surpassed by today's rods because of continued improvements in the material.

Rod length is also important in saltwater fishing, and the advent of graphite has extended the average rod length. For most fly fishermen, an $8^1/2$- to 9-foot rod is best. There are longer rods, such as $10^1/2$ feet, available. Rods that are longer than 9 feet, however, require extra effort to move through the casting arc. Longer rods also mean more air resistance; a day of casting with a longer rod can be quite fatiguing. Overall, a 9-weight rod that is 9 feet long is the best choice.

Whatever rod(s) you select, fighting, or extension, butts are a must. Saltwater fish are powerful, and it is impossible to hold the rod away from your body while fighting them. Fighting butts enable you to rest the rod on your stomach or thigh without your body interfering with the reel's work. Make sure the extension butt is comfortable (ball-shaped ones work great) and not too long. If it is too long, the butt may catch the line when casting for extra distance or while it streams out when following a hooked fish's path.

Line choice somewhat depends upon personal preference; however, some type of weight-forward line is necessary. You can use the standard weight-forward line or a shooting head. Some weight-forward lines are designated "saltwater-tapered," or weight-concentrated at the front of the line (usually in the first 25 feet). They can be more difficult to handle than standard weight-forwards. Floating lines work well for fishing flats species and species that hit on the surface, such as redfish. Slow-sinking or sink-tip lines can, however, be useful in flats when you need to get your fly down quickly.

Factors to consider when selecting a reel include rod weight, line capacity, the hand you use to reel, drag and direct drive or anti-reverse preference. The reel should be large enough to accommodate not only the line but at least 200 yards of backing—even smaller saltwater fish can rip off a lot of backing. Extra backing also helps you gain more line with each turn of the reel handle when fighting a fish. For larger fish, you should have more than 200 yards of backing because big fish take more line and all fly reels have a 1-1 retrieval ratio.

The hand used for reeling depends upon personal preference. Usually, an angler uses his stronger hand.

A good drag that functions smoothly and surely is essential. Most of today's saltwater reels have sound drags. This is partly because lightweight alloys provide more internal space for gears without making the reel too heavy. Most saltwater drags do not make noise.

Other tackle items include backing which is usually 20-pound-test dacron line, leaders and tippet materials, flies and containers and a stripping basket.

Saltwater fishing requires special knots. The Bimini-twist knot is difficult to tie yet essential, according to the masters in the field. The Albright knot, Huffnagle knot and several other special-purpose knots will link various parts of your line and leader together. Loops, such as those formed with a surgeon's knot, are often used to connect leader to tippet, tippet to shock tippet and even line to backing.

Monofilament can be advantageous when used as backing. It has some "give" or stretch that can help absorb the power.

Saltwater equipment requires special care. Reels in particular demand attention because they contain residual moisture from the leader, line and backing. Your equipment should be thoroughly cleaned with soap and warm water, rinsed, dried and stored in areas where it will be free from mold, rust or other deterioration.

Fishing The Surf And Shoreline

It is exhilarating to stand at mid-thigh depth in splashing, roaring surf, savoring the sounds and smell of the sea, and it is even more rewarding if your casts produce some action. Unless there are visible feeding fish, working flies in the surf requires some basic understanding of the potential location of fish. Deep cuts or sloughs will most likely hold gamefish; this is where you should concentrate your casts. Move from place to place, much as

This bluefish took a streamer in the surf. Bluefish are just one of the species found in the surf's deep cuts and sloughs. Surf fly fishing can be rewarding and refreshing.

you would wade a stream, until you find action. There are several fish species that can be caught in the surf during certain seasons. These species include bluefish, "puppy drum" (small redfish), striped bass, sea trout and many others. Streamers work best when you're fishing the surf.

There are other saltwater fishing methods you can execute from shore or by wading. Jetties are widely known as fish attractors. In some cases, they are placed specifically with sportfishing in mind. You will need a stripping basket to prevent line from grinding and fouling up on the rocks that form the jetties. One way to work a jetty is to hop along the rocks while casting parallel to the shore. These probing casts should range in distance—some should be close to the rocks and others should be a long way from shore. The majority of fish usually are found near the ends of jetties or where the jetties meet the beach; however, anywhere pockets exist or standard water-patterns change will be potential fish-holding locations.

It is also possible to fish from low-lying docks and piers found in bays or along man-made channels and intracoastal waterways. In these situations, cast outward from your "perch," concentrating on any visible structure including the shoreline. Then "fan" out your casts to cover as much water as possible from one spot. Once all the water has been covered, move to another casting position.

Another inshore fishing method involves bays, estuaries and similar "inlet" waters. These areas can be fished from shore or by wading, although most fly fishermen work parallel to the shore in a boat. As always, look for structure that attracts fish.

Afloat In The Salt

A boat enables you to cover a lot more water. It also elevates you, allowing you to pinpoint fish location more easily. Some signs of possible fish location are wakes, panicky baitfish, schooling activity and gulls splashing into the water. Places where two channels or conflicting currents come together are attractive holding spots for fish, too. Moving water usually means moving food. Accordingly, tidal channels near inlets are also attractive. (An anchor can help in moving-water situations.)

Another approach to boat fishing is moving along slowly while making probing casts. This can be particularly productive in bays with shoreline vegetation, in inland waterways or around man-made fish attractors, such as docks and bridges.

Schooling fish present unique problems. After spotting a school, move quickly without spooking the fish. If you can determine the school's direction, position yourself in front of the school, drop your anchor and begin casting.

16

Fishing The Flats
And Tackling Billfish

Saltwater fly fishing can be done in deeper, off-shore waters, as well as in the flats. Both of these approaches involve special gear and, possibly, geographical situations. This chapter covers the basics pertaining to both approaches. Although saltwater fly fishing is not as common as freshwater fly fishing, it is a growing trend and an exciting adventure—both in the flats and in deeper water.

Looking at acre upon acre of shimmering white sand, punctuated by greens, golds and blues, and covered by a mirror of crystal clear water, flats fishing has no comparison. While gazing in enchantment, anglers constantly are hoping for a flicker of movement or a hint of a shadow that will reveal their prey. Fishing the flats is not a game of numbers; it is one of constant anticipation and rare triumph.

Fly fishing for billfish requires brave anglers. The sport is still in its infancy, so there is a great deal to learn in all its areas—equipment, flies and techniques. Exploration and experimentation are vital to its success.

The Flats

Several decades ago, Joe Brooks, one of the great names in fly fishing, wrote persuasively and poetically about the phantoms that roamed the flats. Today, flats fishing is probably the fastest growing method of saltwater fly fishing. The flats have the vibrancy and vitality of ocean life in panoramic form ... and often in only a

Flats fishing is the fastest-growing area of saltwater fishing. Not only does it offer beautiful scenery but it also demands extreme skill; the flats are both picturesque and challenging.

Fishing The Flats And Tackling Billfish   181

few inches of water! This is one of the most demanding fly-fishing methods, but it is extremely rewarding and satisfying.

Fish are most likely feeding in the flats; they are often so alert they seem wired. This is because of the environment's exposed nature. The angler must be observant, prepared to make accurate casts within seconds and successfully cope with strong winds. In return, he may be rewarded with anything from a 4-pound bonefish to a 100-pound tarpon.

Most anglers fish in the flats by sight: They spot their quarry, then cast to it. When a storm or some other condition has created turbid water, however, blind casting is required. There are certain tactics that will attract fish, such as laying out chum lines; however, your first step should always be finding fish.

Some fish, such as bonefish, are ghost-like or "translucent," making it difficult to locate them. Polarized sunglasses (brown-tinted lenses seem to work best in the flats) and a wide-brimmed hat that shields the eyes help reduce glare from the sun. Both are extremely helpful in locating flats fish. When looking in the water, concentrate on the bottom.

Elevation helps in spotting fish. Many flats boats are now equipped with platforms that make poling easier and act as a "lookout tower." When visually searching for fish, turn your head back and forth in a steady, scanning motion to cover 180 degrees of water. Look for any type of movement that indicates potential fish location. Sometimes, there will be surface indicators; occasionally, you may even see a tail or dorsal fin. Disturbances in the sand, or "muds," from feeding or possibly fleeing fish are also quite noticeable. The alert flats fisherman always looks for patches of discolored water. These patches often indicate a school of feeding bonefish.

Keep the sun at your back while watching for any signs of life. Sharks and stingrays will be found in the flats if food is available; often a "puff" of sediment off the bottom reveals their presence. Big rays often kick up food from the bottom, attracting smaller fish to dine on this moving chow line. Bonefish, permit, barracudas and other flats species may be in the general area, too. Scurrying crabs or baitfish can also be a promising sign.

Reacting When You See Fish

Stealth rules supreme in the flats. Engines—even trolling

Polarized sunglasses and a wide-brimmed hat are extremely helpful in locating fish in the flats. They help shield your eyes from the sun's glare off the water.

motors—should not be used in the shallow, calm water. You should also conduct casual conversation in muted tones and avoid clanging, banging or scraping noises in the boat. Sneakers, deck shoes or other foot wear with rubber soles should be worn in the boat. Once you spot a fish, estimate the cruising fish's direction and speed. Then, you will need to make a split-second judgment on where the fish and your fly will intersect, but avoid casting into the wind. You may have to maneuver your boat in order to have more favorable casting conditions.

The ideal cast puts the fly down several feet in front of the fish and slowly brings it across the fish's nose with stripping action.

While searching for fish, most experienced flats fishermen hold the fly in their hand with some line trailing and some in neat coils at their feet or in a stripping basket. Once you spot your

The poling/sighting platform in the back of this boat will help the guide spot fish. Elevation is an asset when searching for fish in the flats.

quarry, you need to execute a modified roll cast while releasing the fly from your hand; shoot quite a bit of line on the initial backcast and present the fly on the forward cast.

Shooting line on the backcast can be difficult. You can execute a false cast before delivering the fly. With patience and experience, you will hit your target in the flats.

Fish Found In The Flats

Bonefish. Although bonefish are difficult to see, they are great fly-fishing quarry. Bonefish can be found in abundance, and they seem to be hungry constantly. Anglers who can cast 60 to 70 feet quickly and have mastered the double haul (see Chapter 7) will have an advantage when fishing for bonefish, as well as most denizens of the flats.

There are several fly patterns available that imitate foods preferred by bonefish. The most popular pattern is Dan Blanton's Crazy Charlie, which imitates a crustacean. Epoxy patterns (made with hot glue) have become popular in recent years; however, they are more difficult to cast than smaller flies tied with feathers.

When you see or feel a take, raise your rodtip, hold on and let the reel do the work. Bonefish will basically hook themselves on any pattern you use.

Barracudas. Hooked in the flats, barracudas are powerful, acrobatic and altogether fun fish. Furthermore, this species grows to be quite large—2½- to 3-foot barracudas are common. In short, the barracuda is a sizable and eminently worthy opponent for the saltwater fly fisherman.

These voracious killers with razor-sharp teeth can be quite difficult to see if they are lying perfectly still; however, their black tail and black spots along the body are noticeable when they are moving. Barracudas are spooky fish requiring long casts. These long casts can be difficult to execute with wire leader (their teeth will sever monofilament line unless the fish is hooked at the edge of the jaw).

Casting streamers, then stripping them back quickly, is the standard approach for fly-fishing barracudas. Some tinsel within the pattern is beneficial.

Surface poppers also take barracudas. Cast a popper within the fish's range (but not too close), then pop and gurgle the bug—the more noise the better. Runs of up to 200 yards are not unusual!

Permit. Permit can be caught on fly rods in deep water by jigging streamers; however, most anglers prefer "real" permit fishing—in the flats. Permit hit flies but not readily. In fact, some fly fishermen who have caught scores or even hundreds of bonefish are still waiting to land their first permit.

The McCrab is the best fly pattern for permit. It imitates a crab (a primary food source for permit) and has hooked more of the species than any other fly-fishing offering.

Incredibly powerful and able to use their wide bodies effectively in a fight, permit are capable of severing a leader on coral almost instantaneously or exhausting 200 yards of backing without slowing down. They are also extremely spooky fish, sometimes fleeing the flats for no particular reason.

Redfish. Known locally by various names—redfish, puppy drum (small redfish), drum, spottails, spottail bass and channel bass—this species is found in abundance from the Massachusetts coast southward all the way to Mexico. The culinary craze for Cajun-blackened redfish has decreased its populations; however, stringent regulations in size and number limits, as well as outright bans on commercial fishing in Louisiana and other states, has caused a turnaround in numbers.

Fly fishermen who have caught largemouths with popping bugs will find the transition to redfish relatively simple. The same popping bugs (only smaller) can be used for redfish, although a lot more noise and commotion are recommended when working them in order to catch this species.

Redfish are often found in water so shallow that their tails show. This is a real asset when stalking this species; however, make sure you are looking at redfish tails (their color and rounded shape are clues)—not the tails of mullets which frequent the same waters. Shallow waters can be difficult to fish from a boat, although airboats and specially designed flat-bottomed craft are used. Wading is possible, but use caution—it could be mud flats.

A spottail weighing 10 pounds or more can take out a lot of line, and you may even connect with a 25- to 30-pound fish. Make sure you have plenty of backing for the fight.

Sea Trout. Sea trout, or weakfish, inhabit the same waters as redfish. They will sometimes hit small popping bugs, but small red-and-white streamers are the most effective. Shrimp imitators also work well. Unlike redfish, sea trout limits run as high as 25 to

Permit are considered the ultimate challenge in the flats. They spook easily and are extremely powerful. The McCrab fly pattern is a favorite for taking permit.

30 fish in some states! If possible, use a 6- or 7-weight rod. The lighter tackle matches the sea trout's size and strength.

Tarpon. "Jumping" a tarpon, which describes the hookup and inevitable series of jumps that immediately follows, is an incredible thrill. If you do everything right, including "bowing" (lowering the rodtip to the fish) as the fish jumps to ease line tension and the hook holds, you will be in for the fight of a lifetime—especially if the tarpon weighs 50 pounds or more.

Most tarpon fishing is done by sight in clear, shallow (8 to 10 feet) water. They can be caught, however, on heavy sinking lines in deep holes. This type of fishing takes place primarily in the early spring when the fish begin their annual migration into the Florida Keys. Once the fish move into the flats, the sport enters a new dimension. Anglers must hide along the edges of the flats

Tarpon are spectacular fighters. These fish take small flies, even though they are large fish. Most fly fishing for tarpon is done by sighting the silver kings than casting to them.

188   Complete Angler's Library

until tarpon are spotted. Then comes the challenge of positioning and casting.

Even though tarpon are large in size, they hit small flies. When tarpon are in feeding moods, the angler's biggest challenge is getting a solid hookup. Tarpon usually just suck the fly in. The time for hooksetting is after the fish turns back down. Waiting this second or two can be difficult after seeing a huge fish take your fly only 45 feet away!

If you manage to wait long enough, it is important to set the hook not once but several times. The tarpon's mouth is almost armor-plated, and getting a hook through it can be a real task—make sure your hooks are razor-sharp at all times. There are several tarpon fly patterns, and, unlike permit (which are very selective), tarpon are drawn to various colors. The Stu Apte tarpon fly, named after the man who designed it, is a vivid blaze of red and orange. The popular Cockroach pattern is, of course, black in color. Both flies work extremely well. Tarpon are moody fish, hitting everything one day and ignoring the finest presentation the next. This results in a challenge that attracts hordes of fly fishermen to the Florida Keys and to more remote destinations, such as Costa Rica and Belize.

Billfishing

Unquestionably, the most spectacular saltwater species caught on a fly rod is the billfish. They are powerful fighters when hooked, exceedingly difficult to catch and a true "trophy of a lifetime." Ernest Hemingway, in his powerful and timeless tale *The Old Man and the Sea*, wrote of the billfishing obsession. Zane Grey spent much of his life and literally millions of dollars (earned from his best-selling Westerns) in the quest for billfish. Once fishermen discovered it was possible to take billfish on a fly rod, the challenge became a fixation with a small but growing cadre of anglers determined to do what was once deemed impossible.

Fly fishing for billfish began in the 1950s. Most of the sport's historians credit Doc Robinson for the fly-fishing breakthrough. Others, including the legendary Lee Wulff, Billy Pate, Lefty Kreh and Jack Samson, followed in Robinson's footsteps.

Since the time that Robinson landed his first sailfish on a fly rod, fly fishing for billfish progressed immensely. Along with improvements in equipment, non-technological discoveries have been a major part of this process. Anglers have determined the types of flies and presentations that work best on billfish.

The quest for billfish remains a rare charted fly-fishing frontier—only a few hardy pioneers venture into the deep blue for this monstrous species. This is mainly because the expense of billfishing is beyond reality for many anglers. You need to charter (or own) a boat of considerable size and invest quite a bit of time and money to pursue these fish.

Even with standard tackle, billfish will not be hooked, much less landed, every time out. Those difficulties and uncertainties are multiplied, perhaps several times over, when using fly-fishing gear. Nonetheless, those who have been fortunate enough to know and savor the thrill of catching a billfish on a fly rod consider it the consummate fly-fishing experience.

Types Of Billfish

Sailfish. In one sense, sailfish are a species ideally suited to fly fishing. They will chase teasers (a strip of a fish's belly or a whole fish used to lure the billfish into the angler's range) and readily hit flies. Their mouths, however, are so tough that it's difficult to embed a hook. Once the sailfish "feels" a hook, a spectacular battle begins.

Sailfish have been caught from quite small craft; however, the sportfisherman class of boats are best. Any center-console craft that offers sufficient casting room can also be used; outriggers are removed from one side to give ample casting room. Although sailfish can be caught more easily trolling with a fly rod, International Game Fish Association (IGFA) rules require casting for records. The IGFA regulations also mandate that the boat's motor be in neutral when the cast is made.

Manipulating the teaser bait is vitally important. The angler must get the fish within casting distance, remove the teaser from its path at the precise moment and present the fly. The sailfish should be within 30 to 40 feet. Where the fly goes, as opposed to how far it goes, is critical. The ideal fly location is a bit to either side of the fish, so the sailfish takes the fly in the corner of its mouth. The hookset usually happens from the simple impact of the take.

Most experienced fly fishermen use 12- or 13-weight rods with matching shooting-head, fast-sinking lines. Reel performance and

Billfish are probably the most challenging saltwater fish caught on flies. This sailfish, hooked off the coast of Costa Rica, executes a magnificient leap after taking a fly.

Fishing The Flats And Tackling Billfish   191

This fly assortment represents common patterns for catching sailfish. Double-hook streamers and large, deep-faced poppers work best. Sailfish streamers should have cork or Styrofoam in front of them to make them popper-like.

line capacity are critical in billfishing. There are a few reels on the market capable of holding several hundred yards of backing. These reels can endure the sizzling, powerful runs of large sailfish and even marlin.

Sailfish fly patterns are either double-hook streamers (double hooks are legal under IGFA rules; trebles are not for fly-fishing records) or larger poppers. Most of the streamers have some cork or Styrofoam directly in front of them, making them popper-like lures. Noise is attractive to sailfish, so deep-faced poppers that produce plenty of noise and commotion are recommended.

Using proper knots is essential when fishing this powerful species. Connecting 80- or 100-pound shock tippets to flies and leader and linking backing with the monofilament directly behind the line can be extremely difficult. Anglers should read and research information before starting their sailfishing adventures. They should also fish with a fly fisherman experienced in fly fishing for billfish.

Marlin. Chartering a decent marlin boat with the necessary crew and purchasing top-notch equipment are expensive. This is why few anglers have caught marlins. There are a lot of blanks in the IGFA record book under the marlin category. These empty spaces show that no one has caught marlin using certain pound-tests of tippet.

The nature of a marlin's mouth (and this is true of sailfish, too) presents a major problem. The hook usually encounters hard bone and cartilage—not soft, pliant flesh. Anglers need hooks that are so sharp they could dig into a fingernail—even though they are only 4/0 or 5/0 in size.

As with sailfish, teasers are used to attract marlin. The teaser can be an artificial creation or a bait such as a whole mackerel.

=17=

Overlooked Freshwater, Saltwater Species

Literally dozens of less renowned species can be caught on flies. Most fish consistently landed on standard tackle are fair game for flies, except for a few saltwater species that are too big or found exclusively in deep waters. If you are using the proper technique and have the right flies, fishing for these offbeat species can be exciting. This chapter covers some species, but it is not comprehensive.

If there is a species in your area that is plentiful yet receives little attention from fly fishermen, you have a unique opportunity to explore!

Neglected Freshwater Species
Catfish. Over the last couple of decades, the catfish has emerged from oblivion and into extreme popularity. Outdoor magazines contain several catfishing articles, a National Catfishing Hall of Fame exists and catfish tournaments are set up on a regional level in the South.

Fly fishermen, however, have not hopped on the catfishing bandwagon. Only a select few know that these back-alley brawlers of the watery world are a worthy adversary. Channel cats, in particular, are a great fly-fishing quarry, especially in streams where they can be caught in shoal areas during warm-weather months by wading fly fishermen. In lakes, catfish can be caught around riprap or, during certain seasons, in shallow water. In tailraces, catfish congregate in deeper pockets and eddies below turbines to look for

This hefty channel cat was caught on a fly rod. Although catfishing has gained popularity in many fishing arenas, most fly fishermen do not consider the catfish's potential challenge.

Overlooked Freshwater, Saltwater Species

chopped food. This is an excellent opportunity for the fly fisherman, too.

Catfish are basically bottom feeders; therefore, it is essential to get the fly down to the bottom. Streamer-fly patterns work best, especially minnow, crayfish and lizard imitators. Catfish are frequently found in murky water, so they use their sense of smell in locating food. You may want to use a catfish scent on the streamer (there are many catfish scents available). Incidentally, chumming also seems to work well for catfish. A favorite chum is commercial catfish food.

Whitefish. Rocky Mountain whitefish are widespread in Western streams. Many fly fishermen detest them because they feel that whitefish hurt resident trout populations and are an ugly nuisance. Whitefish, however, rise readily to dry flies and, once hooked, provide exciting action.

Whitefish will hit just about any pattern that appeals to trout, including dry flies, nymphs, wet flies and streamers. Keep your hook size small, though, because the whitefish's small sucker-like mouth cannot take a big fly. Whitefish are generally less selective than trout, but they are not pushovers. Catching whitefish requires decent casting skills, proper presentation and a fly resembling something they would eat. A hefty whitefish (16 to 20 inches) taken on a fly will fight a real battle. Even though this species is quite bony, smoked whitefish (large ones are best) is a delicacy.

Shad. In coastal rivers with annual shad spring spawning runs, fly fishermen can have some thrilling action. A shad hooked on a light fly rod is chained fury! Although it may seem dull before a shad strikes, the angler is compensated in the end with the shad's excellent fighting qualities.

The most productive shad patterns include sparsely dressed flies tied on Sproat hooks. The body is usually wrapped with tinsel, and bright colors, such as red or yellow, are used for the hackle. Attractor beads may be used at the end of the leader, although they make casting more difficult.

Casting is not a major factor in shad fly fishing. Anglers just need to get the fly into a pool where shad are located (using enough split shot to keep the fly suspended at medium depth in the current) and wait. Sometimes imparting a wee bit of motion helps, but the current usually provides enough motion. Basically, this type of approach could be called "stationary trolling."

Shad have great fighting ability once hooked. Popular shad fly patterns, shown here, include sparsely dressed flies tied on Sproat hooks with tinsel bodies and bright-colored hackles.

Patience is the key. Sooner or later a shad will smack your fly, probably out of irritation, and the fun begins.

Carp. Carp are universal victims of bad publicity; however, a fly fisherman will immediately abandon all the misconceptions and become an outspoken press agent touting the fish's virtues after he hooks one. The reason is simple: A carp of any appreciable size (and they can reach rather large sizes) hooked on a fly will battle fiercely.

Finding a fly that appeals to carp can be difficult. These fish are strictly plant-eaters, so standard, insect-imitating patterns will not work. A small fly resembling a tasty tidbit of algae, for example, is best.

One highly effective approach, which can be used in small ponds or during the spawning period when carp concentrate in large reservoir backwaters, is "vegetarian" chumming. Throw a few handfuls of coarsely ground cornmeal or crumbled fish pellets made from grain by-products or cotton seed into the water. This should promote some feeding activity from carp. At this point, cast a small, sparsely dressed nymph amidst the feeding fish and let it sink slowly toward the bottom. The second your line slightly moves or twitches, set the hook.

Bowfins And Gars. Gars are probably the most hated of all freshwater fish, primarily because they prey on sportfish. The voracious feeding habits of gars and mudfish can be used to the fly fisherman's advantage. These fish will strike readily, but setting the hook can be difficult. Their bony mouths turn hook points, and their needle-sharp teeth cut monofilament. Because of the gar's greed, however, you can literally catch these fish using a fly rod without a hook! This requires the use of a "rope fly." Take a short length of braided nylon rope and unravel it. (Yellow or orange colors work best.) When the gar strikes, its myriad teeth become entangled in the rope strands, which work like Velcro at the end of your line.

Gars are powerful fish. In large rivers, they can reach lengths of 4 to 5 feet. You will need a heavyweight rod and a high-performance reel if you plan to fish these destructive and unloved fish.

Bowfins have similar foraging habits—they will eat just about anything. These fish prefer muddy bottoms, hence the nickname mudfish, and like to stay away from currents. Streamers fished slowly in backwaters and shallow sloughs work well.

Walleyes. Walleyes are immensely popular among anglers using conventional tackle; however, they receive little attention from fly fishermen. In some aspects, the species is ideally suited for fly fishing. For example, walleye strikes are often quite subtle, so the fly rod can help detect them.

When it comes to the main ingredient of a shore lunch or a delicate fish chowder, the walleye is superb. The key to catching walleyes on flies is understanding their habits. During early spring when they make their spawning runs out of lakes into large rivers, walleyes can be found in quite shallow water. Bright-colored streamers are most effective at this time.

During most of the year, walleyes spend the daylight hours in the depths and move into shallower waters to feed at night. They do not like light. They also prefer rocks and gravel over muddy

Walleyes are easily caught on bright-colored, weighted streamers in the spring. Fly rods help in detecting their subtle strikes.

bottoms. On gloomy, overcast days, you can sometimes find them in shallower water during the day. The most productive walleye fishing, however, is done at night. They can sometimes be caught on the surface with popping bugs, and patterns imitating small frogs, a favorite item of the walleye's diet, work great in late summer and early fall. For the most part, you will do better beneath the surface, and the flashier your streamer the better. Another good approach is using a fly with a small spinner blade. The flashing blade worked near the bottom of inshore lake areas or streams attracts walleyes.

Other Freshwater Species. There are countless freshwater species that can be caught on flies. Anyone who has done much dry-fly fishing for trout knows how readily chubs, creek minnows and other "pests" take flies. When you move up to their larger cousins, such as fall fish, mooneye, goldeye and herring, you can have some real fun. Even freshwater drum and redhorse suckers can be induced to take flies, although catching them requires considerable patience.

Saltwater Species

Because saltwater fly fishing is still in its developmental stages, there are numerous species that will readily strike flies. It has been

Fall fish and many other so-called "trash" fish are anything but trashy when hooked on a fly-fishing outfit. These fish can provide a day's fishing excitement.

emphasized that a major part of fly fishing's intrinsic appeal is the opportunity it presents for innovation. If a saltwater species spends time in comparatively shallow water and is taken on standard tackle, it can probably be caught on flies, too.

Snappers. Under the best circumstances, mutton snappers are spooky and skittish. This is especially true in the flats where they are sought by fly fishermen. Snappers fight fiercely if hooked and are abundant in many areas. They also are great eating.

Some fly fishing for mutton snappers is done in the Florida Keys, and the epoxy fly is an established favorite. Short, quick movements of a fly that has been cast in front of feeding fish is the standard method of presentation. Long casts and a stealthy approach are important.

Jack Crevalle. When it comes to pure spunk, jack crevalle rate among the best gamefish species. They are awesome fighters that make long, searing runs and refuse to give up. The fish's broad body and powerful tail are partly responsible for its fighting activities. This species responds readily to flies and poppers. Whatever you cast, fly movement is essential. Work poppers with lots of noise, and strip streamer flies as fast as possible.

Jack crevalles are extremely widespread; they are available in tropical climates throughout the world. (This fish is not the best when it comes to eating, which helps explain its abundance.) One of the best ways to catch jack crevalle is to find them in schools smashing bait. If you locate them in this situation, a strike is almost guaranteed. Be sure you have at least 300 to 400 yards of backing. Once you hook a jack crevalle, you will understand why some seasoned fly fishermen actually tend to avoid them. They are powerful fish!

Snook. Snook love shallow water, can be found easily and take various flies readily. The species is also widespread. The Florida back bays and mangrove alleys, for example, hold plenty of snook. Their preferred habitat can present a problem: Snook have the tendency to wrap around roots and snap off your presentation.

Ambush spots around islands or mangrove-lined shores are an ideal location for snook. They will hit poppers or streamers readily, although most anglers prefer poppers because they don't need to worry about hang-ups in underwater vegetation. The poppers should be fairly small and worked the same way as when fishing largemouth bass—give them occasional twitches instead of noisy, repetitive pops. Snook are spectacular fighters, often coming completely out of the water several times immediately after they're hooked. Those in the 3- to 6-pound class are the most common fly-rod fare, but larger ones will hit.

When fishing snook, use a heavy shock tippet; they have sharp gill plates capable of cutting ordinary monofilament. Once you hook a snook, put some muscle in fighting the fish for the first few minutes—their instinct is to head for security. Once you get them away from their home, it should get easier.

Dolphins. Dolphins have beautiful hues of black, gold and green. They are abundant in warmer offshore waters throughout much of the world and can be caught readily on flies. Anyone who has the wealth and inclination to go after billfish will most likely encounter dolphins, or dorados. The problem with fly cast-

This healthy snapper was caught near Key West, Florida. Fly fishing for this species is extremely challenging; snappers are easily spooked.

ing to dolphins is that they move very quickly. The most common way to catch a dolphin is to first hook it on spinning tackle. The entire school will follow their hooked buddy, and a fly or popper cast into the midst of the school will get an immediate response. Often this tactic can be repeated again and again.

Other Species. There are many other saltwater fish that can be caught on flies: smaller sharks, coho and other salmon waiting to enter the spawning grounds, cobia, roosterfish, wahoo, yellowfin, bonito, amberjack and the exotic species of distant locales such as those in Australia's Great Barrier Reef and "back door" buddies like the humble sheepshead. All of these species—and many more—await the fly fisherman who is willing to test new waters, try new flies and explore new frontiers.

Enhancing
The Fun

=18=

Tying Your Own Flies

Tying and designing your own flies is one of fly fishing's "fringe benefits." There is something particularly pleasing about deceiving, hooking and landing a fish with a fly of your own creation. Some fly fishermen find tying flies so entrancing and relaxing, they actually prefer it to being on the water!

Fly-tying has even become a specialized art form. Famous masterpieces sell, like paintings, for premium prices. Framed flies are increasingly popular decorative items in the dens of sportsmen; it is also common for flies to appear in limited-edition books authored by noted fly-tiers. These flies fall into the category of "sporting collectibles."

Aside from the aesthetic and therapeutic aspects of fly-tying, producing your own flies can save you considerable money. Flies are not cheap. Even small trout flies or popping bugs for bream retail at $1.25 to $1.50; larger or more complicated flies, such as those used for salmon or steelhead, can cost several dollars. The materials used in tying your own fly cost pennies. If you ignore the time put in at the tying bench, your potential savings will add up rather quickly.

Another plus to tying your own flies is the versatility it provides. You can bring dozens of patterns to a stream only to encounter a hatch you can't match! If you have a small streamside tying kit and are proficient at fly-tying, you can match the hatch in a matter of minutes.

Streamside fly-tying kits enable anglers to match the hatch in minutes. Using flies of your own creation brings special satisfaction and excitement to the sport.

Tying Your Own Flies

Hundreds of books have been written about fly-tying collectively containing instructions for at least 10,000 patterns! This figure represents only a small percentage of creatures that fish eat. In other words, the number of potential fly patterns is limitless.

Acquiring Fly-Tying Essentials

Fly-tying can be learned from manuals, anglers experienced in the skill or formal classes. Many fly-fishing shops conduct fly-tying seminars hoping you will become "hooked" and buy materials from them in the future.

Every fly-tying kit, whether basic or highly sophisticated, will have four basic elements: tools, other implements, a good hook selection and tying materials. The tools are pieces of equipment and accessories you use repeatedly, whereas materials are bits of fur, feather and man-made materials from which the infamous fly is actually created.

A Fly-Tier's Tools

Most of your initial investment in fly-tying will be purchasing good tools. There are five essential tools: vise, scissors, bobbin, hackle pliers and bodkin. The first four should be made from quality steel that will last for years; almost any sharp-pointed object will work for a bodkin.

The vise is the most important tool. It should be adjustable for height and equipped with an adjustable clamp. It should also have adjustable jaws that can accommodate hooks as small as No. 20s.

The scissors will need fine points suitable for working with tiny bits of hackle or performing other cutting and clipping chores with precision. They should be strong enough to handle stiff material, and large finger holes are important.

The bobbin should have a long, smooth barrel; rough barrels can cause abrasion and breakage when using delicate thread. The bobbin's tension-adjustment apparatus should be made from quality steel.

Hackle pliers are available in many styles. Those with one rubber jaw and one serrated steel jaw work best.

The best available bodkin is free throughout most of the country. It is the needle of a honey locust tree. The bodkin applies the head cement (a quick-drying glue) to the fly for the finishing touch. Bodkins are also used to remove the hackle or other mate-

The lure of the vise is a real and persuasive one. It is the most important fly-tying tool.

rials that have accidentally wound under the thread. Bodkins, whether thorns, dissecting needles found in biology laboratories or commercially made ones for fly-tiers, also help work out monofilament knots. For that reason, many anglers carry them in their fishing vests.

Other Fly-Tying Implements

As you might suspect, fly-tying has more than its share of gadgets. Most can be useful, but they are not essential. These non-essential implements accelerate the tying process, simplify it or aid in producing more attractive flies. A good fly-tying catalog will list these items, as well as many other accessories.

At the top of most experienced fly-tiers' "non-essential" list is a whip finisher. This little device wraps thread more rapidly and tighter than your fingers. A hair stacker is beneficial when working with hair flies. You place deer hair, elk hair, calf's tail or other hairs (not furs) in this slender tube (with lid) and jostle to "stack" the hair. In other words, you even all the hair tips so the finished hair-tied wings will be even.

Beeswax or dubbing wax helps spin dubbing onto tying thread; head cement is then used as a finishing glue. Clear fingernail polish or lacquer can replace head cement if you're desperate. Other handy items include a bobbin cleaner, dubbing twister, small pliers, a file, a material clip and a half-hitch tool.

Hooks

Hook sizes used in fly-tying vary considerably—from huge 5/0 or 6/0 used for saltwater flies to tiny No. 28s used for diminutive midge or baetis patterns. The numbering system for hooks can be a bit confusing. For plain numbers, hooks get smaller as the number becomes larger. For example, a No. 2 hook is much larger than a No. 12. When a slash and zero (called an aught in hook terminology) are added after a number, the process is reversed. Thus, a 5/0 hook is larger than a 2/0.

Hooks come in various styles and shapes, including shank length, assorted types of eyes and different gaps (the distance between the point and shank). There are now even eyeless hooks on the market! The turned-down eye is used on virtually all dry flies and most other patterns. Sometimes, steelhead and salmon flies, as well as saltwater species flies, use a looped eye because it's stronger. Other hook features are wire weight, hook flexibility, styles (such as Sproat, Viking and Limerick) and specialty hooks with crooked shanks for poppers. There are few absolutes in hook choice, although you will want a long shank hook for streamers or patterns imitating lengthy insects, such as grasshoppers. An ant or beetle imitation may require a hook with a short shank. Choose hooks that seem practical to you, "field test" their performance in the water and use the ones that work best.

Tying Materials

There are four basic categories of fly-tying materials: thread, body materials, hackles and wings and tails.

Threads hold the fly together. They come in various colors, strengths, sizes and coatings (waxed and unwaxed). Nonetheless, two or three basic threads are sufficient. A spool of 3/0 monocord and a spool of 6/0 nylon are best. The monocord is strong and heavy; it works well for beginners because it doesn't break easily. Once anglers gain some experience and develop good tying skills, monocord works best for tying flies on No. 12 or larger hooks. For smaller hooks, use 6/0 nylon thread.

Body materials are used for tying the body of the fly. Furs are the most widely used body material, although synthetic materials

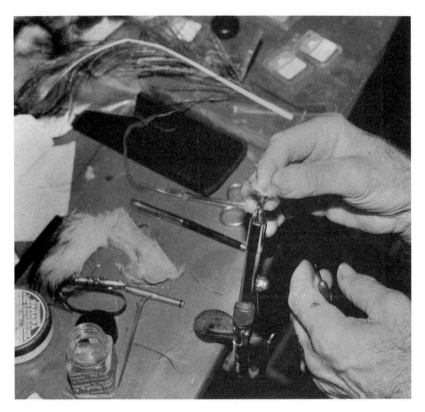

From odd bits of feather and fur come crafty deceptions that catch fish. There are four basic fly-tying materials: thread, body materials, hackles and wings and tails.

are becoming more popular. Furs are now available in every hue of the rainbow, as well as their natural colors. There are also pen-like applicators, which enable you to apply your own colors. Yarn is also a common body material for sinking flies. Antron, a synthetic yarn that glitters in the water, and tinsel are widely used, and chenille is yet another synthetic type. Anglers sometimes use lead wire with fly bodies to help get the fly down quickly; herls from large birds, notably peacocks and pheasants, are also popular.

Hackles are feathers taken from the neck area of various birds. Rooster hackles are the most common. The neck feathers of hens, as well as numerous wild birds, such as grouse, quail, pheasants and even grackles, can be used. Hackles are usually classified for wet flies, nymphs and streamers or dry flies. Dry-fly hackles are more expensive because prime neck feathers that are stiff and

Tying Your Own Flies

Dragonflies are an important food item for trout and bass, as well as other species. They are a real test of skill for the fly-tier.

shiny are required; sinking-fly feathers can be soft and webbed in the center.

There are many materials that work effectively for wings and tails. Wings are usually made from two matching sections of a bird's flight feathers (mallards or turkeys are popular birds for this). These are frequently called quills, although the wing material is cut away from the quill. Flank and breast feathers from waterfowl and turkeys are also used as wings on dry flies. For streamers, dyed marabou is widely used. Deer and elk hair are also used on dry flies because they float exceptionally well. Calf's tail, or kip tail, is also popular for hairwing flies. This is the material commonly used for tying wings on the extremely popular Wulff patterns. Longer hairs, such as bucktail, work well on streamers; fox tails are commonly used for beautiful steelhead and salmon flies.

Obtaining Your Own Tying Material

An incredible array of fly-tying materials is available at retail outlets; many materials can be obtained from nature, too. You will most likely need to purchase peacock feathers or an exotic rooster neck; however, the enterprising fly-tier is also a peculiar scavenger. Road kills are often the butt of jokes, but fly-tiers consider them serious business.

Hunters will have an advantage in obtaining natural material. For example, the wing feathers of wild turkeys are perfect for grasshopper and cricket wing patterns while the tail feathers and breast feathers can be used as hackle. Pheasant and grouse feathers are coveted prizes, and the thought of getting feathers from a male wood duck is enough to bring tears of joy to a serious fly-tier's eyes. In truth, about anything that flies, whether waterfowl or upland game, has potential.

Deer and elk, as well as other hunted animals, bring fly-tying benefits. Strips of rabbit fur still attached to the skin make great pulsating streamers. Squirrel tails, ground hog (woodchuck) hair and even 'possum belly can be put to good use. In fact, opossum fur is a great substitute for calf's tail.

19

Tricks Of The Trade

lmost every experienced fly fisherman has "secrets." Some have secret holes; others have specially favored productive waters. Most anglers protect the detailed information leading to the whereabouts of these holes and waters like the key to Fort Knox! These same anglers probably hold other secrets that have nothing to do with cherished streams or hidden lakes.

Secrets may not be the correct word to use here since these types of secrets do not relate to withholding information or knowledge from others. These "secrets" are tidbits of wisdom, carefully accumulated over the years from rugged experience, that are so deeply ingrained in the fishing character of the individual who possesses them that he is unaware of their importance. They are his stock in trade—the tricks that set him apart from the ordinary angler.

Veteran fly fishermen have expertise that is worth sharing, especially with beginners. Anglers must be eager to learn. Don't be afraid to ask questions, always keep an open mind and seek revelations rather than waiting for them to come to you.

The Angler As Predator
Humans have the mental and physical capacity to be the consummate predator, and becoming a predatory angler is often overlooked. Equipment won't make you one, nor will loads of money that enable you to fish remote, fish-filled waters. The answer is a

Becoming a predatory angler is important in fly fishing. Fly fishermen should learn to seek fish first, then stalk.

Tricks Of The Trade

proper frame of mind. You must want to catch fish!

The key to being a predatory angler is developing good stalking techniques. It has been emphasized throughout this book that wading without spooking fish, keeping a low profile and avoiding the creation of shadows that reveal your presence are all important elements of fly fishing. These are also tactics used in the neglected art of stalking fish.

In its simplest form, stalking involves hunting individual fish. These fish are usually feeding when they're spotted with the help from gulls, polarized sunglasses or rise forms. Anglers need to find fish without revealing their own presence. Casting to a specific fish in a given spot is almost always preferable to blind casting.

Finding fish is only one element of stalking. Stalking is also a constant awareness of the water. The ability to be an intruder in the water world without being intrusive is also critical. Anglers who creep and crawl, as well as study and scan slowly instead of rushing along blindly, are invariably successful. An angler who wears out the knees of his waders first is a smart angler.

Predation is also a game of patience. Impatient anglers are often unsuccessful anglers, especially when they face a situation where catching fish is difficult. The wise fisherman will watch and wait, change flies endlessly and try every possible alternative in order to catch fish.

Finally, be willing to improvise when stalking. A little common sense, the ability to think and plan before casting and the willingness to "stoop to conquer" will benefit you. Success and stalking may not be synonymous, but they do go hand in hand.

Catching Impossible Fish

Never be afraid to try unorthodox tactics or offbeat angling approaches when ordinary techniques fail. Using tandem rigs when fishing for panfish and other species can be deadly, and it eliminates patterns that won't work twice as fast.

As a predatory fisherman, you should know techniques that can catch so-called impossible fish. These fish are often difficult to catch because of their location. You will need to examine the conditions and determine the best way to get the fly to the fish.

Adventurous wading often gets the fly into an "impossible" place. Similarly, the "nothing ventured, nothing gained" philosophy corresponds to catching tough fish. Anglers do not know if

Stooping down low when stalking fish is beneficial. In fact, anglers who wear the knees out of their waders first are usually successful anglers.

certain lies are impossible to reach until they make a few casts. Sometimes, the impossible can be rendered possible by using special techniques. For example, if casting to a specific spot in a stream is impossible, use some bark or a leaf to ferry your fly into the promised land. A twitch of the wrist at the proper time places the fly before your quarry.

Removing the word *impossible* from your angling vocabulary may involve more than what country singer Hank Williams Jr. calls "an attitude adjustment." Overcoming obstacles and rising to challenges are the hallmarks of an exceptional fly fisherman.

Hooksetting Secrets

Getting the hook solidly set can vary considerably according to circumstances; however, there is one constant that cannot be overemphasized: razor-sharp hooks. Always check your hook for sharpness before making the first cast of the day. This can be done by pulling the hook point across your thumbnail. If it doesn't "dig in," you need to sharpen it with a file or hone. You should also check your hook periodically during the day's fishing. Frequent contact with the bottom, catching a number of fish or bouncing a misjudged cast off a boulder can make a hook lose its sharpness and lose fish.

These considerations also apply to leaders and tippets. Check your terminal equipment regularly for any hints of abrasion, wind knots or other problems that weaken it. Hook sharpness and tippet testing are matters of equipment maintenance.

You should never cast until you're ready to set the hook. Do not move and cast at the same time, especially in rough water; mind your slack and keep the rodtip low for maximum leverage when a strike occurs. There will be times when this is not possible with a fly rod; however, you can still set the hook well if your slack line is under control by pulling briskly on the line with your off-hand. If overhead limbs prevent you from conducting an upward sweep of the rod for hookset, keep the rod low and sweep it parallel to the water's surface. Whatever the situation, exert hooksetting pressure in the opposite direction that the fish is facing.

Two of the most common faults on visible strikes when the angler is alert and properly prepared are setting the hook too quickly and hitting the fish too hard. Knowing how and when to set the hook requires premeditation. Prepared anglers will achieve the desired result: a dancing rodtip and pulsating line.

Fishing Where There Are Fish

Sharp hooks and proper hooksetting techniques are important to successfully catch fish, but nothing is more important than getting your fly before the fish. Anglers must learn to find the "strike zone." Reading the water and understanding streamer or nymph depth placement are critical factors in fly placement. Although the strike zone's size varies with things such as water clarity and temperature (it is usually much smaller in winter and expands as water temperatures reach optimum levels), fish will frequently feed instinctively if the fly is placed properly.

Creating an artificial situation that forces fish to change their position also works. A fly drifting by repeatedly can convince fish

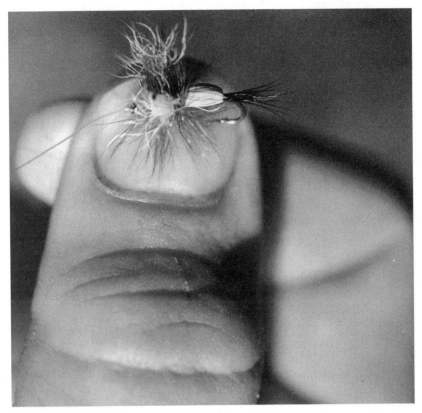

Sharp hooks are essential in fly fishing. The sharpness can be checked by pulling the fly across your fingernail.

that a hatch is occurring. Fish will also strike out of irritation. Whether you vex or coax them, the object is to get them feeding. Most of the time, creating your own strike zone is not necessary. Careful observation, a willingness to alter your techniques to fit situations and resorting to trial and error when all else fails will eventually put you in the strike zone.

Fishing In Foul Weather

Another trick of the trade is fishing in inclement weather. Rain, sleet and snow usually ensure less fishing competition. Numerous companies manufacture clothing and gear that provide comfort in bitter weather.

In cold weather, fish do everything in slow motion because of their lowered metabolism. When air temperatures are really cold,

Tricks Of The Trade

you cannot use dry flies (if it is too cold for insects to hatch or fly, fish will not focus on the surface for food).

Rain brings renewal and acts as a catalyst for "dream fishing." A spring shower or summer thunderstorm can cause a water temperature change in streams that creates an upturn in feeding activity or sparks a sizable insect hatch. Also, many fish species are sensitive to light, and they will be more active on overcast, drizzly days than on bright, sunny ones. Heavy rains, frequently accompanied by strong winds, blow or wash all sorts of insects into the water. It doesn't take fish long to realize that a feast is floating before them. Likewise, a cool rain after weeks of heat or drought can invigorate fish and infuse them with new vitality. This puts fish, as the English like to say, "on the feed."

Fishing Ethics

Basically, good sportsmanship in fly fishing, as in life, amounts to little more than following the Golden Rule. Translated into angling terms, this means steering clear of anglers who have already taken a position in a pool or stretch of water, sharing the sport with others, caring about the sport's future and, of course, always obeying fishing regulations.

Catch-and-release is an excellent concept; however, there are some negative aspects to releasing all fish of all species all the time. If you keep your catch, it should be utilized on the table. When you do creel a few fish, it is better to keep small or medium-sized ones for eating and release the prime brood fish. Modern technology has made it possible to catch and release the fish-of-a-lifetime and still enjoy a mount on your den wall.

Catch-and-release fishing inevitably raises the related issue of fishing barbless hooks. Using a barbless hook makes releasing fish without handling them much easier. It usually requires grasping the hook shank with a hemostat and giving it a quick flip to release the fish. This reduces the likelihood of permanently damaging the fish. If a fish is so tired that it is unable to swim away after you've released it, nest it gently in your hands and swim the fish upright until it is ready to move off on its own. After all, ethical angling involves developing and maintaining a deep respect for your quarry.

Barbless hooks can be advantageous in other situations, too. The removal of barbs results in less metal to penetrate the fish's mouth. This may improve your hookup percentages. (Also, the widespread belief that failing to keep your line tight will cause you to lose a fish hooked on a barbless fly is wrong. Lee Wulff proved this when he hooked a nice trout and then laid his rod down. Several minutes later, he picked it up, tightened the line and showed that the fish was still hooked. Try it yourself if you are still in doubt.)

Caring for your equipment may not be an "ethical" subject, but it comes close. Mistreating a $500 graphite rod or an antique bamboo one worth several times that amount is more than shameful, it's a sacrilege. You should check, dry and clean your equipment after every trip and take particular care when getting it in and out of vehicles. When the season's over, put a mothball or two in with your flies and make sure everything is completely dry before storing.

=20=

Fly-Rod Trophies: Going For Records

S everal fly fishermen consider any fish a trophy because of the pleasure and satisfaction obtained from catching it. The fly-fishing community also thinks that many anglers are too preoccupied with trophies, so those who use the long rod usually try to steer away from the trophy pit. This attitude has contributed to fly fishing's reputation of elitism.

These arguments have some justification, but this chapter will focus on the practical aspects of trophy fly fishing—not the philosophical ones. Records are public knowledge, and becoming a record-holder offers a great sense of achievement.

Keepers Of The Record Books

Two organizations in the U.S. are primarily responsible for maintaining fish records: the National Fresh Water Fishing Hall of Fame (NFWFHF) and the International Game Fish Association (IGFA). IGFA handles saltwater records. Both provide details including record applications and rules to those interested. For information, write or call NFWFHF: P. 0. Box 33, Hall of Fame Drive, Hayward, Wisconsin 54843; telephone 715-634-4440; or IGFA: 1301 East Atlantic Boulevard, Pompano Beach, Florida 33060; telephone 305-941-3474. State wildlife departments handle state records but do not separate out fly-rod records. IGFA includes freshwater and saltwater fly-rod line-class world records in its annual publication; NFWFHF publishes only freshwater line-class fly-rod world records in its annual record book.

Al Whitehurst set an IGFA fly-rod 16-pound tippet class record with this 54-pound, 8-ounce landlocked striped bass. It was taken from the O'Neill Forebay.

Fly-Rod Trophies: Going For Records

Tips For Aquiring Fly-Rod Record Recognition

Detailed guidelines from the NFWFHF and IGFA will inform you of the record requirements. Many potential record-book fish that are landed never qualify because the angler was unaware of the regulations. If you are devoted to catching record fish, know the printed requirements backward and forward.

Here are some general suggestions that should help anglers trying to set records: First, whether the fish is a bluegill weighing a few pounds or a monstrous tarpon, you need to do virtually everything yourself to qualify for a record listing. You cannot allow another individual to assist you, except when netting or gaffing the fish. For example, if a fish went around a submerged root and an angling buddy helped untangle your line, you would be ineligible to claim a line-class record—even if the fish weighed enough to replace the existing record.

Once you land a potential record-book fish, weigh it as soon as possible. The longer a fish is out of water, the more weight it loses through dehydration. Even those kept alive in a live well will shed a few ounces. The potential record fish should be weighed on a certified scale, such as those found in grocery stores, meat markets and post offices. Make sure the scale has a seal affixed indicating it was checked by an inspector. Only as a last resort should you use a spring-type scale.

When the fish is weighed, there should be two disinterested witnesses present. Make sure you get their full names and addresses. If the fish qualifies as a record, these witnesses will be contacted for verification. Along with the weight of the fish, take its other vital measurements: girth, fork length and total length.

You will also need a professional to identify the fish species. A state fisheries biologist is the logical choice for this task. If the fish is possibly a hybrid, it should be identified by a certified fish biologist or taxonomist. Again, be sure you have the name and address of this person.

Photographs are also important. Color prints or slides are preferable, and the fish should be held broadside. Take photographs from various angles, making sure that the fish is well lighted and that the focus is sharp. Close-ups, as opposed to "grip and grin" shots, are more desirable for record-book purposes.

You also need to save at least 15 inches of the tippet used, and the fly should be left attached. If you used less than 15 inches of

Basic Guidelines For Records

✔ No assistance. Must land fish alone.

✔ Weigh fish on certified scale immediately.

✔ Get names and addresses of two objective witnesses.

✔ Take fish's vital measurements: girth, length.

✔ Have professional identify fish species.

✔ Take color photos of fish (broadside and close-ups).

✔ Save 15 inches of tippet.

✔ Leave fly attached to tippet.

This chart shows some basic guidelines to follow when pursuing a record-book fish. Be aware that this is not an all-inclusive list. If you're interested in record-setting, contact the NFWFHF and IGFA for more information.

tippet (the weakest part of your leader system), the catch will not qualify. The IGFA also has time limits for making record claims. Claims for fish caught in U.S. continental waters must be submitted and in the association's hands within 60 days of the catch; claims for record fish caught elsewhere must be received within three months.

How To Be A Record-Setter

There are up to nine line-class categories for freshwater species (test pounds include 2, 4, 6, 8, 10, 12, 14, 16 and unlimited); some of these classes are open. This is also true for many saltwater species. You will also find that some of the existing records are not particularly big fish. For example, the current standard for bluegills with 6-pound-test line is 1 pound, 1 ounce. In short, if you want your name in the record books, there are a lot of possibilities for many species.

Non-Record-Book Trophies

For most fly fishermen, the real thrust for trophies focuses not on record-book fish but rather on those exceptional in size for a given species and region. The concept of the word *trophy*, after all, is largely a matter of perspective. A 14-inch brook trout is the prize of a lifetime in the southern Appalachians; on Labrador's famed Minipi River, the same fish would be considered an indifferent catch.

Thanks to technological advancements in the art of taxidermy, it is possible to catch a fine specimen, photograph it, release it and still admire it on your den wall! Taxidermists no longer need the actual fish in order to produce a true-to-life mount. They now work with your photograph and special, artificial materials to create an exact replica of the fish you caught.

The process involved is fairly simple—at least from the fly fisherman's standpoint. After you land the trophy fish, take exact measurements of the fish's length and girth. (Do this quickly and gently.) Then take several close-up color snapshots of the fish (compact 35-millimeter cameras produce top-quality photos). These photographs help the taxidermist get the coloration just right, as well as the intricate peculiarities, such as a hooked jaw on a male trout or strikingly vivid lines on a striper.

You may also want to weigh the fish, so its weight can be engraved on the brass plaque that accompanies the mount. The best way to weigh a fish you plan to release is with a pocket scale and landing net. Hook the small spring scale through the mesh of the net and weigh the net and fish together. Then subtract the net's weight from the combined weight.

Catch-And-Release

For fragile and highly pressured species, in particular, catch-and-release has rightly found increasing acceptance in recent years. Every devoted fly fisherman should have, as a part of the overall mental perspective he brings to his sport, a conservationist's conscience. In addition to supporting worthwhile organizations such as the North American Fishing Club, fly fishermen should sustain the precious resources that bring joy to the sport.

Graphite replicas, made from photographs, are becoming the wave of the future in displaying your record catch. This taxidermist is putting the finishing touches on this muskie replica with an airbrush.

There are a lot of pros and cons connected with catch-and-release, and this is not the place for a detailed look at the differing views held on the subject by biologists. There is near unanimous agreement to practice catch-and-release with billfish, trout and Atlantic salmon in waters where they are native and brood fish such as big female bass or large redfish. On the reverse side of the issue, you help panfish populations by keeping some for the pan.

Practicing catch-and-release with a given fish or species is a personal decision. If you intend to release the fish you catch, make every effort to do it properly. There is nothing more wasteful than mistreating a released fish. Use barbless hooks to prevent damage (and make hook removal easier). Do not be concerned with losing fish because of the barbless flies. If you need convincing evidence in this regard, you might want to try an experiment along these

When practicing catch-and-release, carefully return the fish to the water. If it cannot swim away under its own power, hold it upright underwater until it gains enough strength.

lines: The next time you hook an average-sized fish, let it swim for about 30 seconds without any rod pressure. Chances are high that you will find the fish still hooked when you apply pressure.

When releasing freshwater fish, using a net can be advantageous (except when fishing species like pike that can get their teeth tangled in the net). There are nets specifically designed with this in mind. Ideally, nets enable you to return the fish to its watery world without ever touching it. If you must touch the fish to release it safely, minimal contact is best. Removal of the protective, slime layer that coats a fish's body increases its vulnerability to disease and lessens its chances of survival. If you must use your hands, make sure they are wet and that you do not squeeze.

It is also important to quickly play fish you plan to release. One which is completely exhausted is less likely to survive the release than one brought quickly to net and promptly returned to the water. Incidentally, an argument against using light equipment for big fish can be made. You can land a trout weighing several pounds with a two-weight rod; however, it will probably not survive. If a fish is so exhausted that it goes "belly up" when released, hold the fish gently upright while working water through its gills by moving it back and forth in the water.

Although it happens less frequently with flies than with other types of lures or bait, a fish will sometimes take a hook quite deep. Hemostats can be helpful when this occurs. If the hook is embedded in the gills or has literally been swallowed, cut it off and leave the fly in place rather than risking damage to the fragile parts of the fish.

Overall, catch-and-release is the wave of the future for numerous species. Perhaps the late Lee Wulff, an early and staunch advocate of this practice for trout, put it best when he said a trout was too great a prize to be caught only once. Fishermen are blessed in this regard: When they release trophy fish, they give other anglers the chance to experience the excitement, too.

Many highly accomplished fly fishermen may never think about catching a record-book fish or even mounting a trophy fish; however, they most likely have their "dream fish" recorded in their memory, diary or photo album. Treasured memories of titillating moments, whether in concrete form or not, are what fly fishing is all about.

Index

Chinook salmon, 154
Christmas Tree flies, 154
Chum salmon, 154
Cigar grips, 25
Clothing, 64-66
Cobias, 203
Cockroach patterns, 189
Coho salmon, 154, 203
Collapsible nets, 69
Color (line), 34
Coon perch, 137
Cork handles, 24
Crappies, 128, 134-135
Crazy Charlies, 185
Creels, 64, 76
Curve cast, 83, 91
Cutthroat trout, 149-150

D
D-rings, 72, 73
Dahlberg Divers, 162, 164
Dampening, 27
Dance of the dry fly, 52
Darter Bugs, 162
Deer-hair bugs, 128
Desperate Divers, 164
Diaries, 66-67
Disk-drag systems, 32
Distance cast, 27
Docks, 109
Dog salmon, 154
Dolly Varden trout, 151
Dolphins, 201-203
Double-haul cast, 83, 89-90
Double-pawl systems, 32
Double-tapered line, 32, 37, 128
Down-locking reel seats, 25
Drag, 29
Drag system, 30-32
Dropper knot, 104-105
Dropper snell knot, 104
Dry flies, 50, 54-58, 163
Dry-fly attractor patterns, 128
Drying granules, 74
Dubbing twister, 210
Dubbing wax, 209
Duncan loop knot, 96

E
Eastern golden trout, 152
Eel patterns, 60
Either-hand retrieve, 32
Elasticity (rods), 22
Elitism, 14-15
Ethics, 220-221
Exposed-rim spools, 30
Extension blood knot, 104
Extension butts, 176

F
Feeder springs, 140
Ferrules, 24
Fiberglass rods, 20, 21
Fighting butts, 176
Figure-eight knot, 105

Finger-twist retrieve, 60
Fingernail polish, 209
First-aid kit, 71
Fishing the rise, 57
Fixed-framed nets, 69-70
Flash-abou material, 169
Flats, 180-189
Flats boats, 120, 123, 182
Flats hats, 66, 182
Flies, 50-63, 169
Flippers, 121
Float tubes, 120-122, 130
Floating lines, 39, 126, 176
Flotants, 74
Flotation device, 120
Fly boxes, 67-68
Fly shape, 52
Fly threaders, 75
Fly tying, 206-213
Fly-tying kits, 57, 77
Fly-tying materials, 210, 213
Fly-tying tools, 208-209
Food, 108
Forehand cast, 83, 91
Foul-weather gear, 71
Four-piece pack rods, 26
Full-action rods, 27

G
Gallasch, Bill, 162
Gars, 198
Gerbubble Bugs, 164
Gingrich, Arnold, 14
Golden trout, 152
Graphite rods, 20, 22, 176
Gravel guards, 120
Green sunfish, 136
Grips, 20, 24-25, 84
Guides, 20, 22-24

H
Habitat, 108-109
Hackle pliers, 208
Hackles, 210, 211-212
Hair stackers, 209
Halford, Frederick, 54
Hand-twist retrieve, 60
Handles, 24-25
Hard knot, 99
Hare's Ears, 128
Hatching insects, 56-57, 108
Hats, 66
Hellgrammites, 162
Hemostats, 70, 77
Herls, 211
Hexagonal rod blanks, 20
Hip boots, 114
Hip waders, 117
Holding spots, 110
Hook hones, 70
Hooks, 210
Hooksetting, 217-218
Huffnagle knot, 105, 177
Hula Poppers, 164
Humpback salmon, 154